THE BREAD AND ROSES STRIKE OF 1912

THE BREAD AND ROSES STRIKE OF 1912

MORGAN REYNOLDS

PUBLISHING

Greensboro, North Carolina

american workers

THE BREAD AND ROSES STRIKE OF 1912

Library of Congress Cataloging-in-Publication Data

Baker, Julie, 1967-
  The Bread and Roses strike of 1912 / by Julie Baker. -- 1st ed.
    p. cm.
  Includes bibliographical references and index.
  ISBN-13: 978-1-59935-044-8
  ISBN-10: 1-59935-044-0
  1. Strikes and lockouts--Textile industry--Massachusetts--Lawrence--
History. 2. Textile workers--Massachusetts--Lawrence--History. 3. Textile
workers--Labor unions--Massachusetts--Lawrence--History. I. Title.
  HD8039.T42U553 2007
  331.892'8770097445--dc22

                                                2006101826

Printed in the United States of America
First Edition

To Frank, Ashley, and Lauren

CONTENTS

Spinning room workers
(Library of Congress)

Chapter 1

A City at War

Just after dawn on February 24, 1912, armed troops from the state militia assembled outside North Station in Lawrence, Massachusetts. The militia's gray wool uniforms blended into the iron cold morning air as they surrounded the building. Many of the men cupped their hands to their mouths in an attempt to warm them and awaited further instructions. Others glanced warily toward the depot, cradling bayonets in their arms.

The soldiers had been sent to Lawrence with orders to assist local police. Their first task was to make sure that none of the people who were holed-up in the station fled the city on the early morning train.

A few minutes past six o'clock, the crunch of hundreds of boots pounding down the snow-covered sidewalks announced the arrival of the Lawrence police department. Fifty police officers marched through the militia's ranks and made their way inside the train station, where they formed two lines,

The Massachusetts militia was called in to help the Lawrence police in what came to be known as "The Bread and Roses Strike of 1912." *(Library of Congress)*

standing shoulder-to-shoulder in dark blue uniforms, to block all exits. The police wielded long wooden clubs, clearly expecting trouble.

February 24th was day forty-four of the largest, most violent, textile labor strike in American history. Strikers, the majority of them immigrants, huddled on benches in the waiting room inside the station. They wore the humble clothing typical of textile mill workers: long, tattered skirts and faded blouses on the women; ragged pants and threadbare shirts on the men; simple, Sunday-best outfits on the children. Hungry and tired, they had no weapons, except for their anger and commitment.

Because they could not feed their children, the striking workers wanted to send them away from Lawrence during the strike. The town's police chief said he would arrest anyone who attempted to put children on the train. *(Library of Congress)*

The children in the group ranged in age from two to twelve, but worry and malnutrition made them look older. Each child had a piece of paper pinned to a worn cap or thin overcoat that listed his or her name, age, address, and nationality, as well as instructions on where the child was to be sent to live, in another part of the United States, until the strike was over. A white ribbon was secured to each child's clothing in case identification papers were lost or torn off. As the train's scheduled departure time of 7:11 a.m. approached, anxious mothers hugged weeping youngsters.

At 6:45 a.m., Marshal John J. Sullivan, the new commander of the Lawrence police force, marched into the waiting room. This was not the first time strikers had tried to send their children away; two earlier, successful efforts had made headlines in newspapers around the nation. The city of Lawrence, the state of Massachusetts, and Sullivan's own police force had suffered nationwide condemnation for not supplying food, shelter, and safety to their impoverished citizens during the bitter winter months of the long strike.

Sullivan was determined to avoid further embarrassment by preventing another exodus of children. "If any of you women," Sullivan shouted, "attempt to send your children away, I will arrest both you and them."

One immigrant mother in the back of the assembly shouted in broken English, "I zend dem to mine friends! They is mine children, not yours! You mind your business!"

Taking her outburst as a cue to action, a representative of the Industrial Workers of the World (IWW) weaved his way through the anxious crowd to the ticket counter. He purchased forty-six one-way tickets to Philadelphia, by way of Boston, for the strikers' children, and ten one-way tickets for their adult chaperons.

At 7:00 a.m., a station employee announced the train's impending departure. Mothers lined the children into pairs and directed the ragged parade toward the exit door leading to the train platform. The smallest children could not see beyond the blue uniforms of the Lawrence police.

Sullivan again ordered the parents to take their children home or to remain inside the station until the train departed. A Polish woman held firmly to her child's arm. "I want rights," she said, and tried to break through the wall of police. The officers shoved her and her child back inside the waiting room.

Suddenly, the tension in the room exploded. Mothers shouted at policemen in Polish, Russian, Yiddish, and broken English. Fathers shoved and cursed the officers. Police barked orders and fought back. Both sides punched and pounded, kicked and scratched. The children cried as they clung to nearby skirts and hands.

When the riot ended seven minutes later, none of the strikers' children were onboard the outbound train. Marshal Sullivan had arrested fifteen of them, and several parents. The prisoners were forced into the back of a waiting truck.

When the prisoner truck left, several youngsters stood helplessly on the station's platform, confused and scared. Many had been abandoned when police yanked their parents away. Mothers had fought to get off the truck, to reach their children, but an officer beat the women with a wooden club until the truck had sped away.

"Police no good," said one witness. He added a few comments about the police department's disregard of constitutional rights before he was arrested, too.

Minutes later, the truck stopped in front of the Lawrence police station. Word of the morning's events had spread throughout the city and by the time the officers permitted the prisoners to unload, strike supporters had gathered to protest.

The arrested parents were taken inside and lined up behind their children before the local judge. The adults were charged with neglect and with creating a disturbance and locked in jail cells to await trial. The arrested children were driven to a city-owned farm outside of town to live until their parents were deemed fit to care for them.

LAW AND ORDER IN LAWRENCE

This political cartoon depicts the Lawrence police holding back children attempting to leave by train. *(Courtesy of Walter Reuther Library, Wayne State University)*

Representatives of the Industrial Workers of the World (IWW), the labor union that had organized Lawrence's textile mill strike and the morning's exodus of strikers' children, issued a statement accusing the Lawrence police of using brutal force against loyal American workers and innocent children. They vowed that the following Tuesday morning, two hundred children instead of forty would be sent away to escape the violence and injustice.

Details of the morning's train station riot soon reached the halls of the United States Congress in Washington, D.C. Traditionally, the federal government left labor disputes to individual states and industries to resolve. When the federal government did intrude on labor disputes, it normally sided with the industrialists and factory owners, not the strikers.

The news out of Lawrence was so disturbing, however, several congressmen felt compelled to intervene.

"Never before," said U.S. Representative William W. Wilson, "have I heard of an attempt to break a strike by preventing the interstate movement of strikers or their families. Conditions at Lawrence seem oppressive and horrible." Lawmakers scheduled a federal hearing to determine facts surrounding the strikers' imprisonment. Strike participants and city representatives were ordered to Washington, D.C. to appear before a congressional committee.

Days later, in a large room on Capitol Hill, the nation's most powerful legislators listened as Lawrence mill workers described life behind factory gates and inside Lawrence's tenement slums. A sad, disturbing story began to unfold that depicted industrial America as a place where human life was worth little, profit meant everything, and strikes were swiftly squelched with police clubs and militia guns.

During the weeklong hearing, lawmakers learned that the workers who made fabric to clothe families around the world could not afford to buy it themselves, and that mothers and fathers who toiled long hours each day inside dangerous factories did not earn enough to feed their children. They also learned about child labor and how very young boys and girls lived in fear of not meeting production quotas.

Questions that had long been ignored by most politicians suddenly demanded the attention of the United States Congress. These were fundamental questions: Do American workers have rights within their jobs? Do American employers have responsibilities to those who work for them? Does the federal government have a role to play in American industry? Since the beginning of the American Industrial Revolution,

Few children in Lawrence, Massachusetts, had a childhood in the early 1900s. Most worked in the mills to help provide for their families. *(Library of Congress)*

wealthy business owners had insisted the answer to each question was no. But, during the frigid New England winter of 1912, twenty-five thousand angry American workers decided it was time to demand new answers. This time, the United States Congress agreed.

Chapter 2
Building an Industrial City

Until the beginning of the American Industrial Revolution in the late eighteenth and early nineteenth centuries, most families in the United States lived and worked on small independent farms. They raised their own food and made their own clothing and worked on a schedule dictated by the changing of the seasons and the rising and setting of the sun.

With the introduction of new technologies and business strategies, the United States transitioned from a society in which most people worked in agriculture to one in which most labored in manufacturing and mining. During the nineteenth century and into the twentieth, family farms were gradually replaced by cities, where people went to live and find jobs in the new industrial economy. Gone were the days when the work hours were governed by the sun; the day was now regulated by shrill blasts of factory whistles.

The Industrial Revolution allowed for the production and distribution of products faster, cheaper, and in most cases better than ever before. But as the factory system developed, and demands for manufactured goods increased, an unequal relationship formed between those who could afford to invest money in business ventures and those who had only their labor to sell.

The owners of factories, those who controlled the capital, were in business to make profits, which meant they were motivated to push workers to produce more at a quicker pace. Laborers began to find that the machines they operated dictated how fast and hard they worked, and also controlled their wages. Over time, the men who owned the machines and hired the workers became wealthy, and many of those who ran the machines barely earned enough to feed themselves and their families.

The large influx of immigrants to the United States in the latter half of the nineteenth century exacerbated the inequality between capital and labor. For every worker hired, there were usually dozens, if not hundreds, of unskilled immigrants who were willing to take the job, often at less pay and for longer hours. Most mill jobs did not require special skills or knowledge of the English language; mill laborers consistently ranked among the lowest paid employees in the country.

Lawrence, Massachusetts was a perfect example of the imperfect relationship between capital and labor that had developed in the United States by the early twentieth century. The city itself was created to make money when, in March 1845, fourteen of New England's wealthiest businessmen, all members of the elite group known as the Boston

Associates, met at a restaurant in Lowell, Massachusetts, to discuss a bold moneymaking venture.

At the meeting, millionaire Abbott Lawrence proposed a plan to build an entire city devoted exclusively to the production of textiles. The city, he explained, would feature dozens of redbrick factory buildings, all strategically constructed near the waterpower of the Merrimack River. The factories would employ thousands of men and women who would efficiently operate row after row of textile machinery. Such a city, Abbott Lawrence promised, would be a model for the industrial world, and anyone clever enough to invest in its startup would likely reap profits beyond imagination.

The gathered men had several questions. Would the new city resemble the existing textile town of Lowell? It would be bigger, cleaner and more profitable, Lawrence answered. Was

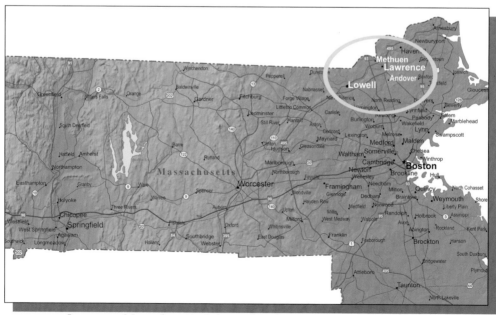

Lawrence, Massachusetts, is located in the northeastern tip of the state.

Abbott Lawrence *(Courtesy of Lawrence Public Library)*

there suitable land along the Merrimack River to build such a city? There was farmland, ten miles north of Lowell, that could be bought for a good price. Where would the workers come from? Don't worry, Lawrence answered, if we build the factories the workers will come.

Abbot Lawrence's vision was huge in scope, but the men of the Boston Associates had the money and political power to make it a reality. Their eighty-member alliance controlled a significant percentage of Boston's banking and insurance interests, as well as more than two-fifths of Massachusetts' commercial ships and three-quarters of the state's buildings.

They also managed 40 percent of Boston's banking capital and one-third of the railroad mileage in the northeastern portion of the United States. Building an entire town around a single industry was a big gamble, but they were powerful enough for the odds to be in their favor.

The Boston Associates agreed to finance Lawrence's ambitious city-building venture. They formed a partnership, the Essex Company, and made Lawrence its president.

In the following weeks, twenty-three hundred acres of rocky Massachusetts countryside was purchased from the towns of Methuen and Andover. Soon huge blocks of New Hampshire granite were transported in to dam the energy-generating power of the Merrimack River, and wagonloads of lumber, bricks, nails, and paint arrived from suppliers around New England to construct the buildings.

Just as Abbott Lawrence had predicted, the workers came. In fact, the supply of workers received an unexpected boost from a disaster taking place on the other side of the Atlantic Ocean. As his city-building plans were formalized, a devastating fungus attacked the Irish potato crop. Potatoes were a mainstay of the Irish diet, which meant that the potato famine left tens of thousands without food. Thousands died from hunger and disease. With no healthy crops to replant, and no aid from their rulers in England, two million poor Irish had no choice but to flee their homeland.

Many scraped together enough money to buy passage on ships bound for the United States. Arriving without food or homes, they were desperate for any work they could get. The newly formed Essex Company eagerly accommodated thousands of them. Irish immigrants were hired to dig and lay foundations, put down bricks, and make streets. They built textile

An illustration on the cover of *Harper's Weekly* shows a woman on the shore of Ireland, heralding relief from America. *(Library of Congress)*

factories, general stores, blacksmith shops, hotels, churches, and newspaper offices. Three years after the dinner handshakes, Lawrence, Massachusetts, was a thriving town with a population of six thousand people.

When the initial construction was completed, most residents sought employment in the city's newly built textile mills. Thousands of men and women were hired to keep the steady clack-CLACK, clack-CLACK, clack-CLACK of factory looms running every minute of every work day.

In the decades that followed, generations of European immigrants and the children of New England farmers came to work in the Lawrence textile mills. Countless bales of cotton and wool were turned into miles of finished fabric.

The operatives (as the workers were called) learned to function as quickly and efficiently as the machines they tended; problem workers, like broken machines, were either corrected or replaced.

Over time, Lawrence's original investors sold their interests in the mills to a new generation of venture capitalists. New owners expanded textile facilities and aggressively recruited workers, particularly from crowded, impoverished European countries.

For millions of European immigrants in the late nineteenth and early twentieth centuries, the words "in America" were a symbol of hope and opportunity. In America, people said, there is food for all who are hungry and jobs for all who want work.

The letters written back home by relatives who had already relocated to the United States often told a different story, however. In America, some wrote, industrial cities are large and dirty and crowded and a man's nationality often determines the type of job he is offered and the neighborhood he lives in. In America, factory work is dangerous and wages are low.

"I came to America because I heard the streets were paved with gold," said one Italian immigrant. "When I got here, I found out three things: first, the streets weren't paved with gold; second, they weren't paved at all; and third, I was expected to pave them."

Despite contrasting accounts of what life in America was like, nearly a million European immigrants came to the United States each year between 1900 and 1914. Most crammed everything they owned into small suitcases and trunks and set out to claim a tiny portion of what would later be known as the "American Dream."

Many immigrants first stopped in large cities like New York or Boston before traveling on to textile towns such as Lawrence and Lowell, to the steel towns and coal mines in Pennsylvania and West Virginia, or to dozens of other places throughout the United States where they heard there was work.

By 1910, the population of Lawrence had grown to almost 86,000 people. Nearly 90 percent of the residents were foreign born or had foreign-born parents. One-half of the city's teenagers between the ages of fourteen and eighteen were employed in the textile mills. With the steady flow of laborers streaming into Lawrence, mill owners expanded their factory operations to increase output and profits. They gave little thought to the lives of workers beyond their factory gates.

By 1912, the city of Lawrence had undergone a radical transformation from its founder's original design. These changes fueled the growing tensions between the city's mill owners and the workers. The single-family homes that had been built according to the original plans of Abbott Lawrence could not accommodate the tens of thousands of new textile mill workers immigrating to the city. Multistoried houses were quickly constructed on every available inch of land and as many families as possible were squeezed into the least amount of livable space. The houses were built so close together that only narrow, dark alleys separated them. There was no space for grass to grow or for sunlight to reach the windows. In a government report prepared in 1912, investigators noted that houses in Lawrence "occupy so fully the lots on which they stand that there is not room to place a garbage can on the same lot with the house."

The area where the mill workers lived was crowded with buildings.
(Courtesy of Lawrence Public Library)

In one section of the city, forty thousand people inhabited less than four square miles of land. In some parts, six hundred men, women, and children crowded onto a single acre. The government report concluded that Lawrence's living conditions were so dismal and overcrowded that "fire risk both to life and property [was] very great."

Conditions were even worse inside the tenements. A single toilet was often used by several families and could be flushed only by carrying water from a kitchen sink. Bathtubs were installed in a few of the buildings, but usually there was no hot water. Coal or wood in kitchen stoves provided the only source of heat during brutal winter months, but the price of a stove was equal to a family's entire three- to five-week income.

The average wage for workers in the steel industry in 1912 was $13.88 per week, and for shoemakers it was $11.42 per week. An unskilled worker in Lawrence's textile mills earned about $6 each week during peak production months. The rent on a small four-room apartment was approximately $3 a week; a five-room place could cost $4. Sixty percent of families took in boarders to help defray the rent. It was common for sixteen or seventeen people to be packed into a few tiny rooms.

With little money remaining after paying rent, few families could afford to eat anything other than bread, molasses, and

Germs, bacteria, and rats lived in the alleys of the slums.
(Courtesy of Lawrence Public Library)

beans. Meat was too expensive except for very special occasions. Fresh milk, at seven cents a quart, was a luxury; most families bought condensed or evaporated milk.

Malnutrition and inadequate shelter were not the only problems. The city's drinking water supply was polluted by sewage and toxic chemicals the mills dumped into the Merrimack River. Malnutrition, disease, and early death were a constant part of life. In the first years of the twentieth century the average life span for a Lawrence doctor or lawyer

Poor living conditions and the pollution of the Merrimack River contributed to shorter life expectancy for mill workers in Lawrence. *(Courtesy of Lawrence Public Library)*

was sixty-five years. A factory owner could expect to live about fifty-eight years. Textile mill workers did not usually live past their fortieth birthday. Thirty-six out of one hundred died before the age of twenty-five. Many succumbed to lung disease caused by the tiny particles of wool and cotton that floated like a permanent New England snowfall inside the textile mills.

In an effort to improve one aspect of life-quality for hundreds of thousands of factory workers, the state of

Massachusetts passed a law, effective January 1, 1912, which prohibited women and children (who had been able to work fifty-six hours each week in the state's factories and mills), from working more than fifty-four hours. The law did not apply to adult male workers, but textile industry owners were compelled to cut their work hours, too, to insure the profit-generating mills operated at peak efficiency.

The law was not popular in Lawrence. Mill owners argued that a cut in operating hours would result in a decrease in output. Mill workers worried that reduced operating hours would lead to wage cuts, which they could not afford. Conditions were already dire. "It makes one's blood boil to hear of whole families . . . existing on $1.10 a day," said a Lawrence businessman.

There was a big, potentially devastating question hanging over each worker's head after the law had been changed. Would mill owners reduce workers' pay by two hours to match the new limitations on work schedules?

A special committee of mill workers met with managers of Lawrence's largest mill operation, American Woolen Company (AWC), just after the start of the New Year to find out if the new law would affect their incomes. The AWC was headed by the most powerful man in the textile industry, William Madison Wood. If William Wood cut wages at AWC, other Lawrence mill owners would do the same.

AWC's managers refused to answer the worker's questions and suggested they contact William Wood personally for an answer. A desperate letter was sent to him, explaining the workers' concerns and pleading for information and a chance to be heard.

Chapter 3

Building an Industrial Empire

I[f a single person could have halted the momentum leading into the massive strike of 1912, it was William Madison Wood. Wood, the son of Portuguese immigrants, was a leader of the nation's textile industry. As president of the powerful American Woolen Company, Wood set policy for dozens of manufacturing facilities and influenced decisions of competing mill owners.

William Wood ruled his textile empire from an office in Boston, but his namesake mill—the Wood Worsted Mill— was both the biggest worsted manufacturing operation in the world, and the largest employer in Lawrence. The Wood Worsted Mill was a massive, redbrick complex built along the Merrimack River. It was six stories in height and boasted more than thirty acres of floor space. Escalators and sixteen miles of aisles provided 6,000 workers with access to 230,000 spindles and approximately 1,500 looms. Each week, a million pounds of wool was transformed

William Madison Wood *(Courtesy of Lawrence Public Library)*

into top-quality fabric for William Wood's agents to sell around the world.

William Wood had risen from poverty to great wealth during his life. It took years of hard work and single-minded determination, but he had accomplished the legendary American Dream, and he believed it was possible for others to make the same journey. Unfortunately for the workers of Lawrence, his life experience, and the philosophy of self-reliance he had developed during his rise, left him with little sympathy for anyone else who could not duplicate his success.

William Wood was born in 1858 in Edgartown, Massachusetts. Little is known about his parents, only that his father was from the island of Pico in the Azores and his mother was a Portuguese immigrant.

When Wood was twelve-years-old, his father died of tuberculosis. As the oldest son in the family, Wood had to drop out of school and go to work full-time to help support his mother and five brothers and sisters. He did not regret this change of fortune. "When my father died," William Wood remembered, "I started to work. That was where my good fortune began."

He was hired by the Wamsutta Cotton Mills in New Bedford, Massachusetts as an assistant in the company's accounting office. The job occasionally required him to run errands to the company's cotton mills and it was on those errands that Wood learned the basics of mill operation. "I asked questions of everybody—superintendents, foremen, operators. . . . From the very beginning, I was curious about the cost of things. . . ."

From his late teens through his mid-twenties, William Wood worked for a variety of textile companies in Massachusetts and Pennsylvania. In each position, he studied the principals of accounting and analyzed business strategies. By 1886, his accounting and cost analysis skills allowed him to command a salary of more than $26 each week. Convinced he understood the textile industry better than most of the men he worked for, Wood traveled to Providence, Rhode Island, in an effort to obtain funding to build his own cotton mill. While in Providence, he met Thomas Sampson, manager of

Frederick Ayer

the Washington Mill Company in Lawrence. The meeting would change the direction of William Wood's life.

The Washington Mill was owned by Frederick Ayer of Lowell, one of New England's wealthiest businessmen. Ayer had invested vast sums of money and countless hours trying to make the mill profitable, but the Washington Mill was a failure.

Sampson was impressed with Wood and offered him a job as head of its cotton-manufacturing department for a salary of $1,800 a year. Wood accepted the job and moved to Lawrence.

For a while, Wood managed the cotton department and then was transferred to the wool section. But he did not improve the financial outlook of the company fast enough to suit Washington Mill's board of directors, and he was fired. Instead of perceiving this as a setback, however, Wood continued to focus on salvaging the struggling business.

No longer an employee, he made an appointment with Thomas Sampson to discuss an unusual strategy for saving Washington Mill and for getting himself rehired. Instead of Washington Mill waiting for buyers to show up on its doorstep, Wood suggested, why not send Wood around the country to gain business clients? Sampson was intrigued with the idea and rehired him at a salary of $2,500 a year, and William Wood boarded a train to begin his new occupation.

The gamble succeeded. By the end of the year, Wood had sold $2 million worth of Washington Mill's woolen goods, and had almost single-handedly rescued the mill. He was rewarded with a promotion to company manager, a salary increase to $25,000 a year, and marriage to Frederick Ayer's daughter, Ellen.

William Wood and his new wife settled in Andover, Massachusetts, in a house they named Arden. It was a sprawling estate nestled in the quiet countryside of northeastern Massachusetts, six winding miles away from the chaos, poverty, and filth of Lawrence. The elegant twenty-room mansion, white with dark green shutters and decorative trim, was not the largest home in New England, or the most elaborate, but it fulfilled the needs of the increasingly prosperous industrial baron and his growing family.

Wood hired a cook to prepare his meals and plan his parties, a gardener to groom shrubs and cultivate the landscape.

He employed a governess to educate his children until they were old enough to attend private boarding schools. On the sixty acres of land, he maintained stables for horses and a pond where his children could swim or ice skate. There was even a building for formal dances and live theatrical performances.

"Dad never was able to do things on a small scale," William Wood's son Cornelius later remembered. He once told his father he wanted a "hen or a goose or a duck—so I can chase it." Wood built three hen houses on the property and filled them with 2,500 chickens.

A nationwide depression in the early 1890s tested Wood's business skills and altered what he expected from employees. As banks across the United States failed, and clothing companies canceled textile orders, Wood developed a labor strategy which allowed him to keep Washington Mill profitable until the economic slump ended.

An expert in cost analysis, he knew he had to cut the cost of producing each piece of fabric. Cheaper production costs would allow him to lower prices, which would allow him to keep making sales during the depression.

The easiest place to cut costs was in wages, but Wood did not want to risk labor problems. Instead of reducing pay, he devised a plan to make them work harder and faster. Under Wood's new system, mill workers who had been responsible for one or two machines were now ordered to manage three or four. Also, the pace of each machine was increased and production quotas were raised.

To quell potential rebellion over the increased workloads, Wood promised financial bonuses to operatives who reached the new quota goals each month. To get more money, however,

Frederick Ayer's mansion now houses the Franco American School, a Catholic elementary school. *(Courtesy of Franco American School)*

the employees had to overcome nearly impossible hurdles. They did not receive extra pay if they missed work during the month or if the other employees in a factory line did not also attain quota levels. For example, a weaver's income depended on the spinner's productivity, and the spinner's bonus depended on the doffer's work.

Wood's strategy was successful in reducing manufacturing costs. Throughout the depression, he drove his employees to their limits and paid them only as much as necessary to ensure they came to work each day. As a result, Lawrence became the most productive textile city in the United States during the economic slump, and the Washington Mill consistently generated healthy profits.

Wood Worsted Mill *(Courtesy of New York Public Library)*

In 1899, Wood merged several textile companies into a single business entity known as American Woolen Company. Seventy-seven-year-old Frederick Ayer was named as AWC's president, and forty-one-year-old William Wood became treasurer. AWC was soon delivering yearly profits of nearly $3 million.

After Ayer's death in 1905, William Wood became president of AWC. His years of single-minded determination had finally paid off with the top job in the textile industry. He was one of America's wealthiest men and he showered his family with vacations, houses, cars, and social club memberships.

An ad for American Woolen Company

Wood's success and vast wealth did not soften his perspective on workers' wages. He ignored the letter written by his workers in 1912. Anyone who worked only fifty-four hours, he insisted, should be paid for fifty-four hours—not a penny more.

Chapter 4
Fighting for Bread and Roses

Wood's refusal to respond to their letter angered the workers. Worried, rightfully so, that their paychecks would be reduced because of the new state law, the workers began to meet. In poorly heated homes, in crumbling neighborhood churches, and on snow-covered city sidewalks, small groups of immigrant men and women, usually of the same nationality and language, met to discuss what to do next. Sometimes the response differed by nationality or ethnicity. The Italians, in particular, were convinced that a strike was the only way to get fair treatment from William Wood and the city's other textile company owners.

A strike is an action workers take against a company if the workers and owners cannot agree about important job-related issues, such as salary and working conditions. During a strike, workers do not do their jobs and do not receive paychecks. Hopefully, if the strikers can succeed in keeping other workers from taking their jobs, factories do not produce products to sell.

Strikes are usually organized and managed by labor unions. A labor union is a group of workers joined together to protect the rights they have in an industry and to serve as a unified force when promoting the interests of their members to companies for which they work.

The words "strike" and "union" were familiar in America in the early years of the twentieth century, but often they had unfortunate connotations. Names of previous strikes and labor conflicts such as Haymarket, Homestead, and Pullman were reminders of conflicts that had led to deadly violence and the defeat of the strikers. During those conflicts, and most others, the government—at the federal, state and local levels—had usually intervened on the side of the owners. Strikes were also unpopular with the general public because of the disruptions they brought to their lives.

The mill owners in Lawrence used aggressive policies over the years to stop unions from developing. They fired would-be strike leaders and drove their families out of company-owned homes and fired employees who spoke out for better treatment. They encouraged competitions and aggravated national, ethnic, and religious prejudices to divide their employees into small groups as a tactic to keep them from uniting. If German workers spoke of striking, for example, mill managers might warn them that newly arriving French-Canadians immigrants could easily replace them. All adult workers were aware that the city was full of youngsters eager to take their jobs.

In the unlikely event a strike was able to form in Lawrence, mill owners were confident it would be short-lived. Lawrence textile workers came from at least twenty-five countries and spoke about forty-five different languages. Almost 50 percent of workers were women and children and the strongest unions, such as the American Federation of Labor (AFL), refused to allow unskilled workers or women to join their ranks.

The Lawrence mill owners were convinced there were too many obstacles for the workers to overcome to success-fully organize a strike. But, on January 10, 1912, a thousand Italian workers assembled at a hall on Oak Street in Lawrence and voted to walk off their jobs if their wages were reduced when the next paychecks were handed out on January 12. Workers from other nationalities made similar decisions. Anger, hunger, and fear had unified the desperate people in spite of differences in nationality, gender, and skill.

Fifteen-year-old Fred Beal was an employee of the Pacific Mills when the strike discussions took place. "The grown-up workers were talking about going on strike if wages were cut. We young people thought it would be fun to strike and made plans to go skating and sleigh-riding . . . all but Little Eva. She and her mother were the breadwinners of the family. Her father had lost an arm at Pingree's Box Shop two weeks after they came from Canada. They sorely needed Little Eva's weekly wage of five dollars and four cents."

On January 11, 1912, the first paychecks under the new state labor law were handed to female Polish weavers in the Everett Cotton Mill. When they opened their envelopes, their wages had been cut by two hours.

"Short pay! Short pay!" The women shouted before stop-ping their machines and walking out of the building.

Throughout the day other workers in other mills were given their paychecks and found two hours of pay had been

STRIKE FRIDAY

All Italian Operatives in Various Mills Will Leave Their Work on Account of Reduction in Pay Caused by 54 Hour Bill---Nine Hundred Attend Meeting

All the Italian operatives in the local mills go on strike Friday night. This action was decided upon at a mass meeting held Wednesday evening and comes as a result of an adverse report from the committee delegated to interview the agents of the various mills of this city.

The grievance is that the pay will be cut to such an extent on account of the new 54-hour law that the operatives cannot meet their living expenses. It is said that they will demand the pay they received before the new law was put into force. Angelo Rocco, secretary of the Italian branch, I. W. W., presided. The hall was filled to overflowing, about 900 Italian operative being present.

Newspaper headline from Thursday, January 11, 1912, announcing the first strike in Lawrence.

deducted from each. By nightfall, two thousand textile mill workers were on strike. But more were to come. The majority of Lawrence's laborers were scheduled to receive pay envelopes the following morning.

An Italian worker named Angelo Rocco sent an urgent telegram to the New York headquarters of the only labor union in the United States that would consider trying to organize the melting-pot of Lawrence textile mill workers—the Industrial Workers of the World (IWW). The telegram read: "Strike on in Lawrence. Your presence required there."

William "Big Bill" Haywood was the founder of the Industrial Workers of the World (IWW).

Angelo Rocco's decision to invite the Wobblies, as members of the IWW were called, into Lawrence's developing strike situation was controversial. The IWW, which allowed immigrants, women, and unskilled workers to join, was also one of the most militant, and most feared, labor organizations. Negotiation and compromise were not part of the IWW's strike strategy.

Founded by William "Big Bill" Haywood in 1905, the IWW's guiding philosophy was that all workers, regardless of skill, gender, race, or age, should be in one massive labor union. When they had gathered all the workers into a single, enormous union, the IWW's goal was to stage a mass strike against all American businesses. After the production and distribution of all goods in the nation were halted, the IWW planned to then seize control of the American economy, destroy the existing capitalist system, and replace it with an economy run by the workers. The IWW's preamble stated:

> The working class and the employing class have nothing in common. There can be no peace so long as hunger and want are found among millions of working people and the few, who make up the employing class, have all the good things in life. Between these two classes a struggle must go on until all the toilers come together on the political, as well as the industrial field, and take and hold that with which they produce by their labor.

The morning after Rocco's telegram was sent, 30,000 workers walked through the gates of the textile mills to begin another workday in Lawrence and to receive their paychecks. "On this Friday morning," said Fred Beal, "the atmosphere

This group of ten- and eleven-year-old boys worked in a spinning room.
(Library of Congress)

at the mill was tense with suppressed excitement. We were not sure that the company would cut our wages. We would know when the paymaster came around at eleven o'clock. The shop was full of rumors."

Fred Beal's manager warned him that if he went on strike, he would never work in the Pacific Mills again and would be blacklisted at the other mills.

> The threat of not being able to get work again in any of the mills made me feel miserable. Where else could I get a job? All Lawrence to me was mills, mills, mills. Perhaps the best thing would be to leave . . . and go West, to be a cowboy like those in the movies. For the first time in my life I felt fear tugging at my heart. Hadn't I promised to help out the family? And now if I went out on strike, I would never get another job in the mills of Lawrence and perhaps . . . from getting a job anywhere. I had to make a decision in thirty minutes before the paymaster came around.

At 11:00 a.m., the paymaster wheeled the paychecks out and stood at the head of a long line of worried workers. The first bunch of envelopes were distributed and opened. The company had cut two hours from each paycheck.

"A tall Syrian worker pulled a switch," Fred Beal remembered, "and the powerful speed belts that gave life to the bobbins slackened to a stop. And then hell broke loose."

As they shouted for a strike, hundreds of angry workers smashed machine gears and windows, cut machine belts and dumped bobbins out of neatly boxed containers. Three men grabbed the mill watchman and forced him to open the mill's locked gates. The strikers, young Fred Beal included, then stormed outside and towards the Washington Mill. They destroyed everything in their path, waving American and

Italian flags and shouting, "Better to starve fighting than to starve working."

The mob charged into the loom rooms of the Washington Mill and began ripping, slashing, dumping, and kicking everything it encountered. Cheers and snow surrounded the mob when it rushed out of the Washington Mill and formed an angry parade that marched off to the sprawling Wood Worsted Mill, and then on to Ayer Mill. New strikers joined along the way and the crowd pushed forward, breaking down doors, stopping the work of other operators, and destroying thousands of dollars worth of William Wood's textile machinery.

City officials sounded the riot alarm, but the strikers surged on towards Prospect Mill, gaining in momentum and number by the minute. When they reached the Duck Bridge, the strikers numbered two thousand. Lawrence police were assembled and determined to keep them back.

Confronted by officers carrying guns and clubs, the mob initially retreated as far as Duck Mill on the North Canal. But then it moved forward again. The police threatened to shoot. A few strikers threw snowballs, rocks, ice chunks, and lunch pails at mill windows in response. The crowd cheered as glass showered down on the street below.

Police rushed into the mass of people with clubs, hitting anyone within reach and the strikers fled. As people scattered, police arrested a few men and charged them with starting the riot. One woman was charged with assaulting a police officer with a knife.

William Wood was at his office in Boston when he received news of the morning's attacks on his factories. He issued a statement to a Lawrence newspaper that down played the

Police officers standing outside Duck Mill *(Courtesy of Walter Reuther Library, Wayne State University)*

strike as an unfortunate reaction to a misunderstood situation. He insisted that he, and other mill owners, were not to blame for the financial consequences of the state's new labor law. He also urged his employees to go back to work.

> The manufacturers are the friends of the employees, and greatly regret that the reduction in the hours of work, which the new law has forced, compels their taking home just that much less money. There has been no reduction in the rate of wages but it cannot be expected that people who work fifty-four hours should take home the wages equivalent to fifty-six hours of work.
>
> When one considers that there are mills in the country running from fifty-six to above sixty hours selling their merchandise in the same market, one can see how impossible it is for the Massachusetts manufacturers to compete against such odds. . . .

There is no cause for striking and when the employees find that justice is not on their side, the strike cannot possibly be long lived. I look for an early resumption of work.

The angry workers were not in the mood to listen to Wood. By 2:00 p.m. of January 12, 11,000 workers had joined the strike. Some were in support of the strike; others were afraid to go to work. Emergency meetings were held at city hall in the offices of Mayor Michael Scanlon, who had become mayor only twelve days before. At the meetings, representatives of the Lawrence mill owners demanded that Mayor

FRENZIED, ARMED MOB DESCENDS UPON MILLS

Operatives Driven From Work—Property Destroyed—Washington, Wood and Ayer Plants in Possession of Strikers Until Arrival of the Police—Officers Have Hand-to-Hand Battle With Rioters at Duck Mill—Clubs Used and Revolvers Drawn—Nearly 12,000 Are Forced Out of Employment

Waving American and Italian flags, brandishing knives and clubs, and yelling like maniacs, 200 Italian strikers descended upon the Washington, Wood, Ayer and Duck Mills this morning, taking possession of the first three plants, and driving the operatives from their work. At the Duck mills the police succeeded in holding the mob at bay by the use of their clubs and drawn revolvers. The trouble was the outcome of several mass meetings held by the foreign mill operatives Thursday night over the decrease in pay caused by the 54-hour law going into effect the first of the year. The pay of the operatives has been reduced, as they are now working two hours less than before. When the 56-hour law was changed to the 54-hour law, the mill owners increased the pay so that the operatives received as much with the reduced hours as they did before. This is what the strikers demand. They want the same pay as they were getting under the 56-hour law. The strike has already forced 12,000 operatives out of work, and it is expected that thousands more will be affected tomorrow.

Destruction followed the mob everywhere. Beginning about 8 o'clock they forced their way into the Washington mill, stopped the motors, cut the belts, tore the cloth, threw the work on the floor, drove the operatives from their looms, broke the electric lights, and pulled down the curtains. Terrible excitement arose and the women operatives became hysterical, many falling in swoons upon the floor. The mob then started for the Wood mill.

Scenes somewhat similar followed. The work was stopped, escalators broken, men and women driven from their work and knives were run through the cloth. The Ayer mill was next stormed. The iron gates on the Merrimack street side were broken open, the power stopped in almost every room, the people driven out and wool and cloth scattered all over the floors. Serious opposition was met when the strikers descended upon the Duck mill. A riot call had been sent in on the fire alarm—box 333—and nearly all of the regular police force had reached the scene by this time.

Officers Turner, Donahue, Morrissey, Fortune, Barry and Howitt were in front of the gates when the strikers arrived at the Duck mill. The officers rushed, large pieces of snow and ice, clubs and even dinner pails were thrown at the police, some striking the officers while other missiles went through the windows. The little band of bluecoats had a hand-to-hand fight in the doorway with the enraged strikers. Finding clubs ineffective the officers had to draw their guns and this caused the crowd to fall back for a moment. Suddenly one rabid talker was raised on the shoulders of his friends. He talked in a high-pitched voice and waved his hands frantically for a few moments. When he stopped talking the crowd again stormed the gates.

Meanwhile Officers Lanen, Casey, Kimball, Woodcock, Cadegan, McCarthy, Gurry, Sullivan, Shikarallah, Roche, Griffin, Hart, Kallaher and O'Sullivan had arrived, some by autos, sleighs and electrics and others on foot. This force succeeded in repulsing several rushes of the strikers until finally the men withdrew across the street and kept up a perfect hail of ice and snow upon the police and at the windows. Hardly a pane of glass was left in the Union street side of the mill.

This was the scene of most of the trouble. Several of the strikers got clubbed over the head by the officers and four or five policemen were injured. Policeman Turner, Jordan and Hart were cut in the face and Sergt. Reardon was also hit and cut. A number of arrests were made.

The portion of South Union street between the Canal and Duck bridges was choked up with humanity during this riot. The operatives of the Wood and Ayer mills, driven from their work, were passing to their homes to this side of the river and were held up by the mob of strikers. Electric cars, autos and teams had great difficulty in getting through the crowd but after the wrath of the strikers abated somewhat, the police succeeded in clearing the street and bridge.

36   The Lawrence Daily American, January 12, 1912

Newspaper headline from January 12, 1912

Scanlon order state militia troops to guard their property. Scanlon and other city officials refused, believing the police department had matters sufficiently under control.

All afternoon, strikers roamed the streets of Lawrence. They passed out flyers to everyone they met asking the strikers to refrain from violence because it would lead to sympathy for the mill owners.

Other notices listed times and locations for upcoming meetings where workers could talk about their worries and make additional plans for the strike. Mayor Scanlon announced he would attend the strikers' meetings to reassure workers that their demands would be heard and to encourage them to return to their jobs.

The situation had spun out of the mayor's control. That night, after darkness fell over the snow-covered city, a train pulled into Lawrence station and a man got off at the depot's wooden platform. His name was Joseph Ettor, and he carried a suitcase filled with IWW union membership applications. He also had a dangerous strategy for winning the Lawrence Strike.

Chapter 5
The Imported Agitator

There were only a few known details about Joseph Ettor before he arrived in Lawrence on the night of January 12, 1912. Ettor was born in New York, the son of Syrian/Italian-American parents, and grew up in Chicago. His mother died when he was nine-years-old. As a young man, he worked in a series of odd jobs: cooper, railroad water boy, shipbuilder's assistant, lumber mill laborer. There was nothing in his history that should have worried government and business officials.

There was nothing about Joseph Ettor's appearance that would make anyone afraid of him, either. When he stepped off the train at the Boston & Maine depot he looked like an ordinary visitor, maybe in town to visit family, or perhaps pursue a business opportunity. He had a round, boyish face, a quick smile, and a mass of dark, curly hair that spilled across his forehead. He was average in height and rather heavy around

Joseph Ettor *(Library of Congress)*

the middle. He liked to wear a red, long-sleeved shirt and a black tie when he traveled.

But to many officials in the United States government, and business leaders across the nation, Joseph Ettor was a dangerous man because he earned his living doing the one thing wealthy industrialists feared above all else: he recruited workers into the militant IWW. Smiling Joe Ettor, as he was called, was a popular speaker at labor rallies because he inspired unskilled workers, mostly immigrant men and women, to believe that they were important. By addressing them in languages they understood (he spoke fluent English, Italian, and Polish and had a good grasp on Yiddish and Hungarian), Ettor convinced the country's overworked, underpaid, immigrant laborers that their opinions counted and that their needs deserved to be met.

His orations were not fiery monologues filled with hate or threats of violence. Instead, Ettor consistently told listeners that the secret to gaining better wages and improved working conditions was to simply stop working: "As long as the workers keep their hands in their pockets, the capitalists cannot put theirs there. With passive resistance, with the workers absolutely refusing to move . . . they are more powerful than all the weapons and instruments that the other side has for protection and attack."

Inspired by Ettor's peaceful and empowering rhetoric, lumbermen in Oregon, steel laborers in Pennsylvania, and shoemakers in New York had staged strikes against industrial bosses. In small towns and big cities across America, hardworking men and women agreed when Smiling Joe said that they had a right to a greater share of the wealth their labor produced.

While Ettor's message and delivery was not violent, government officials and industrial barons were convinced that Joseph Ettor and the IWW were out to destroy the very foundation of the United States' economic system. They were right. The goal of the union was to replace the economic and political system in the United States from one that protected private property first and foremost to one that protected the rights of workers and tried to equalize wealth and income.

The morning after Ettor's arrival in Lawrence, local newspapers embarked on a campaign to discredit the strike. They blamed the strike on people from other cities who had somehow infiltrated the Lawrence mills and instigated the prior day's destruction of property. The outsiders, newspapers declared, were foreigners who were "ignorant and easily deceived and more readily excited" than good, quality American workers who actually lived and worked in the city. They labeled the strike as unpatriotic and anti-American.

When the whistles blew on Saturday, signaling the start of the workday, it appeared that the newspapers had been at least partially right. Thousands of Lawrence's workers walked through the mill gates and started up their textile machines without incident. Many of those who had not received paychecks the day before, quietly waited in line for them, seemingly resigned to accept the two-hour reduction in wages.

There were a few small clashes reported between strikers and nonstrikers in some parts of the city as the morning progressed, but no major fights or destruction of property occurred. By noon, city officials and business owners were optimistic that everyone would be back to work by Monday. Mayor Scanlon scheduled a meeting for 2:00 p.m. at city hall to impress upon remaining strikers that the city was sympathetic to their needs, but would not permit further violence. As a courtesy, he agreed to let Joseph Ettor address the crowd when he finished.

Fifteen hundred workers showed up at the meeting. Mayor Scanlon gave his speech in English. It was a short, but direct address. He asked the strikers not to repeat the previous day's violent protests and reminded them that America was a law-abiding country and that they were expected to obey laws. He suggested that the city council could arrange a meeting between strikers and mill owners to negotiate a settlement. "All that I ask" the mayor said, "is that you remain peaceful and quiet in your meetings and do not congregate on the streets or at the mill gates. If anyone desires to work, let them do so. They have got as much right to work as you have to strike."

After the mayor finished speaking, Joseph Ettor, wearing a wrinkled blue suit, stood before the expectant crowd. When a wide smile spread over his face the audience reacted with deafening applause.

When the cheers subsided, Ettor reminded the city's textile workers that it was their long hours in the mills that produced the nation's supply of cloth, and that it was their labor that made men like William Wood wealthy. He said William Wood did not deserve to grow rich while workers' children starved. Profits, Ettor insisted, should go to laborers, not to men who starved workers into submission. The Lawrence textile mill strike, Ettor proclaimed, was more than a battle over a few cents in a pay envelope. It was a fight to better the lives of all American workers.

"Fifty cents buys ten loaves of bread," Ettor said. "Every one of you has that much invested in this struggle. It is a question as to whether you will get more or less bread," he continued. "Monday morning you have got to close the mills . . . tighter than you have them now. Forget that you are Hebrews, forget that you are Poles, Germans, or Russians. Among workers there is only one nationality, one race, one creed." An enormous cheer erupted. The Lawrence strikers had found their leader.

Ettor then repeated his entire speech in Italian and had others translate it into French, Belgian, Polish and Lithuanian. Each time his words were repeated in a different language, they were accepted with enthusiastic applause.

Immediately after the meeting, Ettor created two committees to organize the strike. The executive committee was charged with establishing meetings, developing strategy, and holding centralized authority over the strike. Twenty-four-year-old Annie Welzenbach was the only female member named to the executive committee. She was a weaver at the Wood

Mill and earned $20.58 a week, far more than most of the other strikers. She had joined the strike immediately after it started, and her fluency in German, Polish, and Yiddish was invaluable in keeping strikers informed and united in the weeks to come.

The other grouping was a general strike committee. It was comprised of representatives from each of the participating nationality groups and from various crafts and jobs inside the mills. Initially, the general strike committee had fifty-six members, but later expanded to sixty. Ettor was elected chairman of the strike's management team.

The next day, January 14, was a Sunday, and in churches all over the city preachers, ministers, and priests urged the textile workers to go back to work on Monday. They argued that any problems between workers and owners were best handled while everyone was calmly doing their jobs and the city was functioning. The churches, like those who worshiped in them, depended on the income generated by the mills.

Ettor, meanwhile, met with the newly formed strike committees. As chairman, he appointed people to be in charge of smaller, subcommittees to deal with specific issues. One group would handle the financing of the strike; a second would ensure the strike received nationwide attention in newspapers; a third would arrange strike meetings, parades, and other events; a fourth would set up relief efforts to ensure that strikers and their families received food and heat-fuel.

Once the basic organizational matters were under control, Ettor granted an interview to reporters who wanted to know the strikers' plans for the beginning of the workweek. Ettor insisted that if any violence occurred when the mills' whistles blew Monday morning it would not be caused by the strikers.

"We desire peace as much as anyone and our men will only act when they are provoked," he said, and then added "but if they are, I cannot stop them."

The formation of the strike committees, and Ettor's comments, were no comfort to Mayor Scanlon. He changed his mind about using the militia and ordered five companies to report for duty that afternoon. It was the first time in Massachusetts history that the state militia was called in to keep peace during a textile mill strike. When militia troops had been used in strikes in other parts of the country the violence had escalated. When the militia was present a single fired shot could start a gun battle that would haunt the city of Lawrence forever.

In a snowstorm around six o'clock Monday morning, five thousand strikers followed Ettor's advice and blocked

State militia were called in to help keep the peace. *(Courtesy of Walter Reuther Library, Wayne State University)*

Strikers are sprayed with water to keep them in check. *(Courtesy of Lawrence Public Library)*

entrances to the Wood and Ayer mills. They lined up shoulder to shoulder and prohibited passage to anyone who attempted to return to work.

It was a standoff that seemed destined to lead to violence, and within a few hours Lawrence was a battle zone. Strikers fought non-strikers, mill guards, and city police, and broke into the Pemberton, Prospect, Atlantic, and Washington mills and destroyed everything within their reach. Police officers arrested more than thirty people and stabbed at least one striker with a bayonet.

Temperatures hovered in the single digits as thousands of angry, frustrated, and scared strikers marched towards the Pacific

MILITIA CHARGE MOB WITH BAYONETS FIXED

Scenes of Riotous Disorder Mark Early Morning Hours in Vicinity of Mills, With Angry Crowd Defying Streams From Fire Hose Trained in Their Faces, and Soldiers Grimly Awaiting Orders to Clear the Streets.

Greatest Disorder in Front of Atlantic Mills Where Great Crowds Gathered--Rioter With Gun Fires Several Times Without Effect--One Man Bayonetted by Soldiers--Twenty-Eight Arrested at Lower Pacific--Watchmen Oppose Crowd at Arlington Gates With Streams of Water--Aid Summoned From Out of Town by Mayor Scanlon--Governor Foss Offers Assistance of the State Forces.

The strike assumed very serious proportions this morning and shortly before 9 o'clock the Militia were called out to aid in quelling the disturbance. At the same time police aid was called for from the neighboring cities. Adjutant General Pearson also ordered the militia to be prepared to come here from Lowell and Haverhill.

Guards are now stationed in the vicinity of all the mills and at the police station. Companies F and L were called out first and an hour later Battery C was also ordered out.

The trouble started early in the morning at the Wood and Washington mills where employes were prevented from returning to work. The crowd then went to the Lower Pacific where the violent demonstrations occured. Trouble followed at the Lawrence Dye Works and at the Arlington mills where windows were broken. One man arrested by special officers was armed with two daggers, a revolver and belt of cartridges.

Governor Foss has offered the assistance of the state force.

STRIKERS RUSH WOOD MILL.

A mob of in the neighborhood of 5000 gathered in the vicinity of the Wood and Ayer mills shortly after 6 o'clock. Their gathering was slow, but their appearance threatening and they filled the air with harsh shouts and wild cheers. The police soon became separated by the press of members and those trying to get into the Wood mill to work were in many cases forcibly prevented from doing so. Captain Sullivan, in charge of the forces at this point, exerted almost superhuman efforts to prevent interference with the people wishing to work.

The crowd continued to grow in size and excitability and only the lack of a leader prevented an outbreak. Petty leaders would spring up from time to time and brief rallies would follow in the middle of the streets, but they were quickly subdued.

As the number of operatives trying to get in to work increased the number of the strikers became stronger and their efforts became centered on an effort to gain an entrance to the mill and prevent by force the starting of the plant. Just at 6:45 at the time when the speed is usually started up, a determined rush resulted in the entrance of about 40 of the strikers who proceeded to the second floor, where they were accustomed to work.

Gates Closed in Faces of Rioters.

A few moments later another and more compact attack was made and a general advance was made against the main gate. A determined stand was taken by Watchman Barry, who succeeded in closing the both doors securely in the faces of fully 50 desperate men. Only three got in at this time and they were promptly taken in charge by the mill officials, all of whom were armed with clubs and cudgels. The first man through the door was Santo Tigaro who claimed to be employed there. He resides at 99 1-2 Common street.

For over an hour the mob howled wilde outside and in the meantime a small mixed riot occurred in the second floor among the strikers who entered first. They attempted to release from Overseer Walter Spurr, but were overcome. They were finally allowed to leave the mill as soon as it was thought advisable to open the doors at 8:05.

* * * * *

40

Newspaper headline January 16, 1912

Mill. Frantic mill managers ordered three fire hoses turned on. As strikers neared the mill's gates, powerful streams of water rushed out to stop them.

"The pressure was so great," remembered First Lieutenant Walter M. Pratt of the militia's Eighth Regiment, "that those in front were knocked down and went rolling over and over across the bridge." As their clothes froze against their skin, strikers threw snowballs and chunks of ice at the men holding the hoses.

In other parts of the city, mobs armed with clubs and revolvers took over streets. They yelled, threw ice, and shattered windows. According to First Lieutenant Pratt, between forty and fifty people were jailed that day, most for carrying guns, knives, and clubs. Many strikers and soldiers suffered stab wounds and injuries from flying objects.

"You may turn your hose upon the strikers," Ettor later told Lawrence officials, "but there is being kindled in the heart of the workers a flame of proletarian revolt which no fire hose in the world can ever extinguish."

"Don't you think, Mr. Ettor," Mayor Scanlon asked him during a meeting at the Lawrence police station, "that you are

Colonel E. Leroy Sweetser, head of the Massachusetts militia

responsible for this trouble today? Don't you think that this is all due to the speech you made at the mass meeting last Saturday?"

"I am responsible for what I do," Ettor replied, "and I am responsible for what I said. I am not responsible, however, for what people do who have been provoked as these textile workers have. I am not responsible for what men do when they have been downtrodden, when their faces have been ground into the dirt so that they no longer resemble human beings."

"I believe," the Mayor insisted, "that if you had not made that speech to the textile workers Saturday afternoon, Mr. Ettor, we would not have had this trouble today. . . . Now if you will call off the men who are making this trouble and will take the first train back to New York where you came

Guards stationed outside a mill *(Courtesy of Walter Reuther Library, Wayne State University)*

from, I believe we can settle this strike very quickly."

Ettor replied: "I shall stay here and do what I can for these people."

Everywhere Joseph Ettor went, he reminded strikers of the importance of unity and nonviolence, but newspaper editors refused to believe he was a champion of peaceful demonstrations. The *Boston Herald* called him an "imported agitator" and the *Boston American* described him as the "instigator of violence."

Believing Mayor Scanlon would seek any excuse to have him arrested, Ettor warned strikers: "They would jail me in a moment if they thought by so doing they could take the life out of the strike. The life of the strike does not depend upon me, and don't forget that."

Mayor Scanlon realized the increasing number of strikers, and their intensity, out matched his local police force. He authorized Colonel E. Leroy Sweetser, commander of the Massachusetts state militia, to take full control over all decisions affecting the mill district. The colonel immediately stationed five hundred soldiers as guards around the mills and ordered searchlights and telephones placed in mill towers. He also ordered sharpshooters positioned inside the towers at night.

As evening settled over Lawrence once again, armed militia patrolled the city's darkening streets. "Things were so unusually quiet that there was a general feeling of suspicion," First Lieutenant Pratt later wrote, "and every one seemed to feel that it was the lull before the storm and that trouble was due at any moment." He was right, but when the trouble arrived Wednesday morning it was unlike anything Lawrence had ever seen before.

Chapter 6

A New Kind of Strike

Around eleven o'clock on Wednesday morning, January 17, in the shadows of the mills where sharpshooters had kept watch through the night from the towers, a crowd of strikers gathered. At first, there were only a few dozen people, then fifty, then a hundred and more. But unlike previous strike gatherings, this time no one was angry and no ice or rocks were thrown or shouts aimed at the mill owners.

Instead, the crowd on Elm Street had an air of celebration. Someone unfolded a huge American flag and a few people marched behind it down the street. Soon others joined in and the small parade became more than a thousand people strong. Sounds of laughter and musical instruments filled the cold New England air.

As they marched, the strikers sang the words to "The Internationale," a hymn which they repeated throughout the strike that was becoming a unifying symbol of workers everywhere:

Arise ye workers from your slumbers
Arise ye prisoners of want
For reason in revolt now thunders
And at last ends the age of cant.

Away with all your superstitions
Servile masses arise, arise
We'll change henceforth the old tradition
And spurn the dust to win the prize.

So comrades, come rally
And the last fight let us face
The Internationale unites the human race.

The parade proceeded past the city common, then onto Union Street to Common Street, picking up more strikers as it wound its way through town. By the time it reached city hall, the procession had grown to three thousand people, by Essex Street it was close to four thousand strong and stretched over four city blocks. Fueled by the partylike atmosphere, the marchers continued beyond the downtown office buildings and then turned towards the river and the mill district, where the militia was waiting.

Soldiers blocked the street and pointed their guns toward the advancing people. Those at the front of the parade were forced to stop inches from sharp bayonet points. The bands fell silent.

A militia captain ordered the strikers to turn back. The strikers refused. The soldiers aimed the points of their guns at strikers' chests. For several tense seconds, each side watched the other, uncertain about what to do next.

Then a car slammed to a stop behind the lined up militia. Colonel Sweetser climbed out and maneuvered himself into the narrow gap that separated his soldiers from the Lawrence strikers. A few of the immigrant strikers removed their hats as a sign of respect.

The colonel looked at the flags the strikers carried and took note of their trumpets and drums, as well as the solemn, sad faces of the men, women and children in the crowd. He realized his soldiers were not facing an angry mob. They had stopped a peaceful morning parade. The colonel ordered the militia's guns lowered and his troops to step back. The strikers applauded and resumed their march. They dispersed shortly afterwards.

Picketers urge mill workers to join the IWW. *(Library of Congress)*

The following day, strikers staged another parade that grew to more than ten thousand participants. Although it was also peaceful, Colonel Sweetser decreed afterwards that parades would no longer be allowed in the vicinity of the mill district.

Optimists who thought the parades signaled a calm strike were disappointed after lunchtime on Saturday, January 20. A rumor spread through the tenements that a large shipment of dynamite had been delivered to Lawrence. No one knew who ordered it or who was planning to use it. Would it be used to blow up the mills? How many people would be killed in such an explosion? How many homes and stores would be destroyed?

Joseph Ettor denied any knowledge of a dynamite plot and advised strikers not to believe it. "If any dynamite is found," Ettor said, "it will be dynamite that was planted by the paid agents of the opposition, the mill officials. They have been driven to a state of desperation and are trying to break up this strike."

With the help of an unnamed informant, Lawrence police soon discovered twenty-eight sticks of dynamite at three separate locations. Some were found in a church cemetery, a few were discovered wrapped in blue paper in the closet of a house on Oak Street, and more were found at a nearby tailor's shop. In the wrong hands, that quantity of dynamite could bring down an entire mill or dozens of tenement homes, potentially killing thousands of people. Police announced that additional sticks were still hidden somewhere in the city.

Ettor insisted that the police and mill owners were responsible for planting the explosives—that it was a plot by William Wood to discredit the IWW. He reassured the strikers that dynamite was not part of the IWW's strategy.

A nervous Colonel Sweetser increased the militia's presence throughout the city. During daylight hours, his soldiers kept people moving; they were uneasy when small groups gathered. During the night, soldiers took turns watching the streets from positions high in mill towers, their searchlights illuminating city sidewalks.

William Wood told Mayor Scanlon that there was no strike in Lawrence, just a state of mob rule. Without mentioning the dynamite, he addressed the issue of wages once again in a newspaper letter to striking employees of the American Woolen Company:

> Our Employees:
> Last Friday many of you left our mills and have since remained away. This action was wholly a surprise to me. I learn from the newspapers that the reason for your staying away is that the company paid you for only fifty-four hours' work; but you know your wages are paid by the hour or by the piece, and as you work only fifty-four hours you could be paid only for fifty-four hours' work.
> I want every man and woman working for the American Woolen Company to get the best wages that the company can afford. I have consulted long and anxiously with the directors and those associated with me in the management. Reluctantly and regretfully we have come to the conclusion that it is impossible . . . to grant at this time any increase in wages.
> You are being advised (so I am informed) by men who are not and never have been employees of this company, and who do not live in this state and are strangers to you. They do not know the history of your relations as employees with this company. But you and I, on the other hand, are members of the organization. We all of us have been getting our living from the company. When the company is prosperous we are prosperous. Your advisors have nothing to lose in the disasters of an unfortunate strike or lockout. You and I have everything to lose.
> (signed) William M. Wood, President

DISCOVERED!

Large Quantity of Explosive Stored in Tenement on Oak St. Ferreted Out by Local Police in Charge of Inspector Rooney of Boston--- Seven Placed Under Arrest in Connection With Seizure.

A large quantity of dynamite and concussion caps wer e located Saturday by a detail of plain clothes men in charge of Inspector Rooney of Boston, and it is thought that it is the first chapter in one of the worst dynamite plots in the history of this country. There is no doubt in the minds of the authorities that the explosives found were in readiness to carry out some of the plots that have been rumored for several days past. It is felt that a number of mills and buildings in this city were marked as targets for destruction. It is confidently hoped that the finding of this supply of dynamite will prevent the carrying out of any such plots, but the vigilance of the militia and the state and local police will be redoubled in an effort to locate any more of the explosive that may be hidden about the city. The find was made in an empty room in the rear of the "Marad Dye Works" at 292 Oak street. The dynamite was hidden under paper and at the time the room was entered no one was there. Seven persons, two women, who were on the premises were placed under arrest and taken to the police station.

* * * * *

Pres. Wm. M. Wood Makes Statement

The following communications signed by William M. Wood, president of the American Woolen company, was received last night.

AMERICAN WOOLEN COMPANY.
Lawrence, Mass., Jan. 19, 1912.
To Our Employes:

Last Friday many of you left our mills and have since remained away. This action was wholly a surprise to me. You sent no notice of what you were intending to do and made no demand. I learn from the newspapers that the reason for your staying away is that the company paid you for only 54 hours work; but you know your wages are paid by the hour or by the piece, and as you work only 54 hours you could be paid only for 54 hours work.

Ever since you left I have heard no word from you or any of you as to what you desire, but I have read in the newspapers that among other things you want your wages raised so that you will receive as much as 54 hours work as you did for 56.

Your thus leaving the mills without notice and without any attempts at a conference is unfortunate all around. Both the company and employes are bound to lose a good deal of money as a result, which neither of us can afford. I am not blaming you, because I realize you were greatly disappointed and that some of you acted hastily and the rest followed; but I want you to see how hard you have made my own position.

I am an employe of the company as you are. As its president I am bound, on the one hand, to take proper care of the interests of 13,000 stockholders. Quite a number of them are employes, and most of them are not rich. Many of them necessarily depend on their dividends for their living just as you depend on your wages for yours. On the other hand, I am bound to look out for the interests of some 25,000 employes. It is my duty to see that each side has a square deal, and I try my best to perform that duty fairly and honestly.

I want every man and woman working for the American Woolen company to get the best wages that the company can afford. You work best for the interests of the company when you are contented, but you must realize the stockholders' interest and see that the business is properly managed. You know we have very sharp competition and if we do not do our work economically our competitors will drive us out.

The last two years have been very discouraging years in our line. The present year being a presidential year is also bad for business. You realize, too, that the hours of labor are shorter here than in other states. If we should pay as much for 54 hours labor as our competitors in other states pay for 54 or even 60 we should soon have to quit. I am not criticising our Massachusetts law, but for the present, you see, it puts us under a handicap.

I have gone over the whole situation with a desire to do my conscientious duty to you and to every one interested in the company. I have consulted long and anxiously with the directors and those associated with me in the management. Reluctantly and regretfully we have come to the conclusion that it is impossible, with a proper regard for the interest of the company, to grant at this time any increase in wages. Trade conditions do not justify an increase.

I ask you to have confidence in this statement and to return to your work. As long as I have managed the affairs of this company, it has never yet reduced your wages, but on the contrary, four times the company has increased your wages without your asking. I say further to you that when the conditions of our business are again such as warrant raising your wages, I shall, again, without even a request, recommend such an advance as circumstances warrant. This proves that I have looked after your interests pretty well in the past. Why should I not have your confidence for the future?

You are being advised (so I am informed) by men who are not and never have been employes of this company, and who do not live in this state and are strangers to you. They are strangers to me also, and I know of them only by report. They do not know the history of your relations as employes with this company. But you and I, on the other hand, are members of the organization. We all of us have been getting our living from the company. When the company is prosperous we are prosperous. Your advisers have nothing to lose in the disasters of an unfortunate strike or lockout. You and I have everything to lose.

I, therefore, as the head of this organization of which we are all members, appeal to you to return to your work and faithfully discharge your duties. I will try conscientiously to discharge mine, and together we will try and create a prosperity for the company which will help us all.

We shall thus end a situation perilous to your interests, perilous to the interests of the company, perilous to the interests of the city–a situation from which nothing but ill feeling and disaster can result.

The Evening Tribune, January 20, 1912

43

The *Evening Tribune* headline from January 20

As the first full week of the strike drew to a close, nearly twenty thousand workers had walked off their jobs. The strike committee had developed a formal list of demands and asked to meet with mill owners but William Wood refused all contact with the strikers. He did not want to recognize the right of the workers to organize into unions. If he met with them he would implicitly be accepting the union's right to speak for the workers. Other manufacturing bosses followed Wood's lead and refused to meet with the committee.

On Monday, January 22, the strike committee responded to William Wood's letter:

To President William M. Wood:
Sir: We are of the opinion that you have had ample time to consider the demands of the men, women, and children who have made the American Woolen Company what it is today.

We, the committee, are willing to meet the officials of the company at any time and submit the grievance of the strikers. You must bear in mind the fact that these men, women, and children have not gone on strike for light or transient causes, but because they could no longer bear up under the burdens laid upon their shoulders. The workers are of the opinion that the only competition left is the struggle among themselves for a miserable job . . . .

You speak of men from out of town who know nothing of the textile industry. We, the committee, would like to know if the militia . . . recently sent into this city, know anything about the textile industry except to bayonet and club honest workingmen into submission.

Here are the demands of the strikers:
- Fifteen percent increase in wages.
- Abolition of the bonus or premium system.
- Double pay for all overtime.
- And no discrimination against the strikers for activity during the strike.

(signed) STRIKE COMMITTEE

The same day that the committee's letter appeared in a local newspaper, strikers organized stationary picket lines in front of the mills. They stood outside as snow fell, holding signs which declared their reasons for striking and singing songs of solidarity and nationality.

"It was a new kind of strike," wrote journalist Mary Heaton Vorse. "There had never been mass picketing in any New

England town. It was the spirit of the workers that seemed dangerous. They were confident. . . . They were always marching and singing."

Colonel Sweetser did his best to stop the singing and to reign in the comradery of the strikers by issuing an order outlawing meetings. "We [the militia] are going to look for trouble," he threatened. "We are not looking for peace now."

While strikers dealt with the militia and police on the streets, the strike committees fought hunger and cold in the tenements. Large kitchens were set up to provide food for families who could no longer afford bread or soup and small allotments of coal were given to those who needed help heating their homes.

Family living in a crowded attic home *(Library of Congress)*

Yet, even with aid provided to them, many people felt the two-week strike had already lasted long enough. Some began to consider crossing the picket lines and returning to work. Others made plans to return to their home countries.

"We came to America thinking it a country of fine prospects," said one immigrant as he prepared to return to Italy. "We were urged to come here by posters spread throughout Italy by the American Woolen Company, describing how mill owners will treat us like their own children. It is a false pretense. We were treated like dogs. Our Italy is bad but your country's textile mills are worse."

Joseph Ettor realized the Lawrence strike needed fresh momentum to keep it going. It needed a hero. He immediately contacted William Dudley "Big Bill" Haywood, one of the original founders of the IWW, and requested that he come to Lawrence to re-energize the weary textile mill laborers.

Big Bill Haywood was not a friendly, willing-to-negotiate organizer like Joseph Ettor. He was loud with a quick temper and a reputation for settling disagreements with his fists. He was five feet eleven inches tall and weighed in at 240 pounds. It was said that when Big Bill Haywood arrived in a town, everybody knew it.

True to the fundamental IWW creed, Haywood believed the answers to all workers' problems rested in the formation of one large union in which all laborers stood united against big business leaders. If violence was needed to change the way American businesses were run, or the way American workers were treated, Haywood supported it. IWW members idealized him; President Theodore Roosevelt called him an "undesirable citizen."

Striker Fred Beal wrote:

> I hadn't realized there was so much misery in America
> until Haywood explained it to us. New York had thousands of
> sweatshops where old women and nine-year old children slaved
> twelve and more hours a day for a pittance. . . . In Pennsylvania
> miners were entombed underground twelve hours a day at
> starvation wages. . . . The South lynched its negroes. . . . IWWs
> were being tortured in Western prisons for demanding bed linen
> and liceless bunks in lumber camps. . . . Even work conditions
> in the Lawrence mills were worse that I thought. [Haywood]
> produced pay-envelopes . . . to prove how low were the wages
> in our mills. How could mothers and fathers raise a family on
> five or seven dollars a week?

As Ettor had hoped, William Haywood became an instant hero to the striking textile workers of Lawrence. When he arrived in the city by train on January 24, 1912, Haywood was greeted by 15,000 jubilant men, women, and children. He cheerfully removed his hat and waved it at the crowd as he stepped off the train. Two bands and a drum corps accompanied him in an impromptu parade to downtown, where Ettor and the strike committee waited.

Unexpectedly, mill owners sent word they would meet the strike committee at Mayor Scanlon's office the night Haywood arrived, at 7:00 p.m.

At 2:00 p.m. Ettor addressed a crowd of ten-thousand people on the Lawrence common. First, he introduced his friend Arturo Giovannitti, poet and editor of the Italian newspaper *Il Proletario*, and then he officially presented forty-two-year-old William Haywood. The crowd cheered wildly and formed another parade in celebration. The addition of Big Bill Haywood, and the promised upcoming

Bill Haywood's arrival in Lawrence was noted by the local paper.

meeting with the textile mill owners, had given them hope that the strike might soon be over.

That evening, as planned, Ettor, Haywood, and the fifty-six member general strike committee arrived at city hall for their meeting with the mill owners. But, instead of finding William Wood and the other mill owners waiting to talk, they were introduced to mill representatives. Then the representatives refused to meet with Ettor and Haywood and demanded to speak directly to individual strikers from each of the city's mills.

Ettor and Haywood were furious. The strikers were united under one union, Ettor told the mill representatives, and would only deal with mill owners through their union representation, not individually as workers. Ettor stated that the strike committee would only agree to meet again if the actual mill owners were present. The meeting was adjourned.

Two days later, William Wood met with Joseph Ettor at AWC's Boston headquarters. Once initial pleasantries were over, Ettor listed the four demands of the Lawrence strikers. Wood refused to comply and asked Ettor to revise them. Ettor said no and Wood declared negotiations were at an end.

"Mr. Wood told me that while I represented twenty-thousand strikers, he represented fourteen-thousand investors," Ettor told strikers after the meeting.

From that point, and until the end of the strike, William Wood refused to meet with Joseph Ettor and the IWW. He also refused to give interviews to newspaper reporters and did not send any more letters to his striking employees. "I was held up to the public as an object of hatred," Wood later complained.

Ettor warned the strikers to prepare for a long, continuous struggle in the days and weeks ahead. Big Bill Haywood left Lawrence to rally support for the strike around the nation.

Although William Wood refused to directly participate in the day-to-day issues brought up by the strike, his company representatives remained very active. Immediately after the unsuccessful meeting between Wood and Ettor, agents of AWC knocked on tenement doors and falsely informed strikers that the strike was over, terms had been accepted, and everyone should go back to work on Monday. Ettor was irate. "If an overseer comes into your house and invites you to betray yourself into being . . . a scab . . . throw him down the stairs!" he shouted during one of his speeches. If anyone did return to work in the mills, Ettor advised, he or she should sabotage the machines. "If they starve us back to the looms, God help their cloth, their yarn, and their looms." In one speech Ettor added an ominous threat: "This town won't be very happy in two days. Something is going to happen."

On Monday, January 29 at 5:15 a.m., 1,500 strikers gathered on Essex Street for a massive parade designed to keep non-striking workers from entering the mills that morning. Ettor was in the crowd, reminding participants against the use of violence.

The strikers were quiet and orderly as the sun slowly began to light the streets. Then, a single streetcar, loaded with workers on their way to the mills, appeared on Broadway Street and headed for Essex. Without warning, strikers began throwing ice and rocks at the trolley. A couple of men managed to climb on top of the trolley and disconnected it from its overhead line and the inside of the streetcar went dark.

"Scab! Scab!" strikers shouted, yanking everyone out of the trolley and onto the street. Workers were punched and hit; lunch pails were kicked away. When another streetcar rumbled into view the strikers headed for it.

Lawrence police failed to get control of the situation. By the time the riot ended, dozens of people were injured, nine strikers were arrested, and sixteen streetcars were damaged.

When a reporter asked Ettor about the day's violence, he replied he did not know anything and suggested that if he had, he would have tried to stop it. Ettor blamed the attacks on mill owners, claiming they had planted rioters in an innocent crowd. A small article in that day's local newspaper predicted Ettor would soon be arrested.

Around five p.m. that evening, just as non-striking workers left the mills at the close of the work day, another riot

BULLET KILLS WOMAN; OFFICER BENOIT STABBED

The climax of the strike situation in this city occurred late this afternoon when a crowd of about a thousand assen
on and Garden sts. and a squad of a dozen policemen was dispatched to the scene to disperse the crowd. The officers broke
again and broke a number of heads. At the height of the trouble about a dozen shots were fired and then the militia boys
more shots were fired and a woman was seen to fall. She was fatally wounded and lived but a short time. She was a resi
Shortly afterward Policeman Benoit was stabbed in the back. He was one of the officers that were engaged in disper
quickly removed to the General hospital close at hand and there it was decided that he was not badly hurt and he was shor
me.

After a conference between the mayor, Adjutant-General Pearson and Governor Eugene N. Foss in the State house this a
to send 12 additional companies of militia here, also two troops of cavalry from Boston and 50 members of the Metropolitan
se troops were immediately despatched to the scene and they will arrive here by midnght.
* * * * *

THE STRIKERS AND THE PUBLIC

There are two distinct principles at issue in the present strike; first, the rights of the strikers; second, the rights of the public. By "rights" in this connection we mean the legal rights which are upon the rights of people to labor, and can only react to the disadvantage of the strikers. More, than that it merely means that any continuation of the course will lead to placing the entire city under

On January 29, the first fatality of the strike happened when Anna LoPizzo was killed by a stray bullet.

erupted at the corner of Union and Garden Streets. Strikers threw rocks and ice at workers and police officers retaliated by attacking the strikers with long wooden clubs.

Not wanting a second out-of-control riot to develop that day, Colonel Sweetser rushed militia troops to the scene to assist. Police formed a line on one side of the strikers and militia formed a line on the other side. Police and militia thrashed strikers with the butts of their guns until the crowd started to scatter.

Then someone fired a gun.

Several women screamed as a thirty-three-year-old woman—a striker—fell to the pavement. Her name was Anna LoPizzo. The strike had claimed its first fatal victim.

Chapter 7
War Measures

On the same day Anna LoPizzo was killed, the Lawrence police apprehended a suspect in connection with the dynamite plot. The suspect surprised everyone. John Breen was a former city alderman and a current member of the school board. One of Lawrence's most prominent citizens, Breen was charged with conspiracy in connection with planting the dynamite.

The next day, Tuesday, January 30, police followed Joseph Ettor and Arturo Giovannitti to the Needham Hotel and arrested them there in connection with the shooting of Anna LoPizzo. Both men had been miles away when the shooting occurred, but were charged with being accessories "before the fact of murder." The accusation was that they had given speeches with the intent to incite a crowd to murderous riot.

The judge hearing the initial case against Ettor and Giovannitti informed them that the charge of being accessories before the fact of murder was equal to being charged with the actual murder under the laws of Massachusetts. If the two men were found guilty, their punishments would be death.

The judge also ruled that, although it was common to allow a person charged with murder to post bail, he would not permit it in the case of the two strike leaders. Ettor and Giovannitti were destined to languish in a Lawrence jail until a trial date was set. William

Arturo Giovannitti

Haywood was called back to Lawrence to assume leadership of the strike.

In the following days, the IWW insisted a police officer had shot Anna LoPizzo and that mill owners used the tragic incident as an excuse to jail the strike leaders. Witnesses came forward who were willing to testify that they saw a militia solder fire the shot, but authorities continued to blame the two strike leaders for the crime.

Uncertain how the strikers would react to the arrests of Ettor and Giovannitti, Mayor Scanlon requested additional militiamen and police officers be sent to the city. Fifteen hundred soldiers, fifty Boston policemen, and eight U.S. Marine sharpshooters arrived to assist local law enforcement. Colonel Sweetser notified the strike committee that if anyone believed the soldiers "are afraid to shoot, they are making the biggest mistake of their lives."

There were no radios or televisions to instantly update the public on national events in 1912. Telegraphs and telephones transmitted some details of the LoPizzo death and Ettor's arrest around the nation, but the newspapers and magazines brought news of national events into American homes. Soon reporters and photographers began to travel to Lawrence to see for themselves what was happening and to report their findings to interested readers.

Until the press began covering the Lawrence textile mill strike, middle-class Americans had little concept of the living conditions of the working poor in the industrial cities. Initially, the strike was viewed by outsiders as an isolated problem between disgruntled workers and business owners in a place not known for having labor troubles. But as photographs

When newspapers across the country began carrying stories about the plight of the mill workers in Lawrence, most Americans were shocked to see such horrible living conditions. *(Courtesy of Lawrence Public Library)*

began to appear in newspapers and magazines around the country, public sentiment shifted in support of the strike. The grainy black and white pictures captured disturbing images of the families who ran the machines that produced fabrics Americans bought and wore. The weary, defeated faces of the fathers and sons photographed only inches away from the menacing bayonet points of American soldiers shocked many middle-class Americans. Other published pictures captured the haunting eyes of mill children, their bodies malnourished and poorly clothed, waving American flags; fire hoses blasting people with water on a frigid New England morning; and parade marchers carrying signs asking for nothing more than enough bread to feed their families.

Through the pictures, the strikers' plight became real, and very troubling. Newspaper editors in distant areas of the country expressed support for the Lawrence textile workers and their jailed IWW leaders. An editor in Topeka, Kansas wrote: "Why not have arrested, rather, President Wood of the American Woolen Company, as an accessory to the murder of a striker? He had as little and as much to do with it as Ettor." The day after Anna LoPizzo was

Anna LoPizzo's funeral

fatally shot, another striker died. Eighteen-year-old Syrian John Ramy was stabbed by a soldier with a bayonet as punishment for throwing ice. Anna LoPizzo was buried on Wednesday; John Ramy was buried on Thursday.

On the same day John Ramy died, mill owners announced that hundreds of workers were returning to their jobs. The textile mills of Lawrence, they happily announced, were operating once again. The clack-CLACK, clack-CLACK, clack-CLACK of looms could be heard minutes after work whistles blew each morning. The mill owners encouraged the remaining strikers to return to work as thousands of their peers had done.

To verify the mill owners' statements, two reporters—one from the *Boston Globe* and another from the *New York Times*—slipped past the militiamen guarding the mill entrances and got inside the noisy mills. As the mill owners had stated, there were rows and rows of textile machines running at full speed—but there were no workers in the rooms. The mill owners were bluffing.

"They say the strike is over," Haywood said when he returned to the city, "but as far as I can see, it is all over Lawrence. Instead of the arrest of Ettor breaking up the strike it has increased it."

Twenty-three thousand workers were on strike as the month of January ended. Including the family members who depended on strikers' pay, 50,000 people—out of Lawrence's population of 86,000—were without any source of income. The IWW claimed that the strike was costing William Wood's mills $14,000 per day in lost revenues, and was costing the state of Massachusetts nearly $6,000 per day in lost tax revenues.

But with Ettor under arrest, two strikers killed, and hundreds of militia soldiers patrolling the city's streets, the strikers' morale was sinking. They had gone without paychecks longer than anyone had expected. Food was limited, fuel was running out, and their children were cold, hungry, and afraid.

The strike committee, with the help of the national IWW union, organized a relief effort. They wrote newspaper advertisements and leaflets and asked for financial aid in speeches around the country.

Help Your Fellow Workers Who Need Bread and Your Support. Twenty-five thousand men, women, and children employed in the textile mills of Lawrence, mostly employees of the American Woolen Co., are out on strike against a reduction in wages that at best was only an average of $5 to $6 a week.

The textile industry . . . pays the lowest wage scale of any industry in America. Workers have dared to rebel against conditions that were unbearable. Because they have dared to assert their manhood and womanhood and determinedly insisted for an opportunity to live by their labor, hired military Hessians have been sent to Lawrence to terrorize the workers into going back to work.

We workers, who have done our utmost share to clothe the world, are now asking the world of labor and all those who sympathize with the cause of the workers for bread.

Contribute liberally. It is our fight to-day; who knows, it may be you tomorrow who will need support.

Issued by authority of the Textile Workers' Strike Committee. Joseph Bedard, Secretary, 9 Mason Street, Lawrence, Mass.

The nationwide pleas for assistance brought thousands of dollars worth of clothing and cash into the city. Unions, private organizations, and individuals sent collectively, on average, about $1,000 a day to fund the strike. The money was used to set up stores, establish soup kitchens, and to provide families with food, clothing, and fuel. But, in spite of the donations, life remained difficult. Soup kitchens could only serve a few thousand a day and the cold Massachusetts' winter made the minimal heat in homes almost unbearable.

Ettor sent notes of encouragement to strikers from his jail cell, but without his constant, reassuring presence many feared the strike would fall apart. The strike committee issued statements asking strikers to remain steadfast in their quest for better wages:

> The strike is won if you, the workers, stay out as you are doing! The arrest of Ettor and the others is simply a proof of the desperation of the bosses. Instead of breaking the strike, it has only strengthened the workers' determination to get what is due them. . . . Attend meetings. Don't be a scab! An injury to one is an injury to all!

Name	Date			Number of union	
				Church	
Address	Floor	Front or rear	Rent	Benefit or savings	
Husband's name	Occupation			Wage Past Present	Mill
Wife's name	Occupation			Wage Past Present	Mill
Children	Age	Occupation or school		Wage	Mill
Lodgers				Room rent	
Aid given Total income				Past	
Date				Present	

A record was kept by the IWW for each family that requested aid.

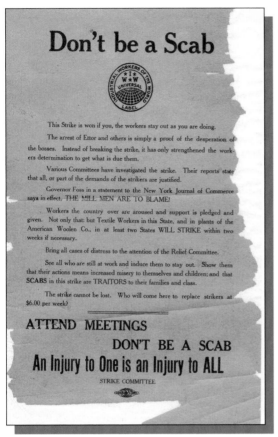

Don't be a Scab

This Strike is won if you, the workers stay out as you are doing.

The arrest of Ettor and others is simply a proof of the desperation of the bosses. Instead of breaking the strike, it has only strengthened the workers determination to get what is due them.

Various Committees have investigated the strike. Their reports state that all, or part of the demands of the strikers are justified.

Governor Foss in a statement to the New York Journal of Commerce says in effect, THE MILL MEN ARE TO BLAME!

Workers the country over are aroused and support is pledged and given. Not only that: but Textile Workers in this State, and in plants of the American Woolen Co., in at least two States WILL STRIKE within two weeks if necessary.

Bring all cases of distress to the attention of the Relief Committee.

See all who are still at work and induce them to stay out. Show them that their actions means increased misery to themselves and children; and that SCABS in this strike are TRAITORS to their families and class.

The strike cannot be lost. Who will come here to replace strikers at $6.00 per week?

ATTEND MEETINGS

DON'T BE A SCAB

An Injury to One is an Injury to ALL

STRIKE COMMITTEE

IWW poster *(Courtesy of Lawrence Public Library)*

Desperate to end the standoff between capital and labor in Massachusetts, Governor Eugene Foss sent two delegations, made up of three state senators and five state representatives, to investigate conditions in Lawrence. One group met with strikers and the other, led by future United States president Calvin Coolidge, met with mill owners. Both sides refused to cooperate.

Public sentiment began to blame William Wood for not doing more to resolve the strike. Frustrated at his bad press, Wood lashed out: "Why make me the figurehead all the time? It isn't my strike. Talk to someone else for a change!"

After weeks without paychecks, Lawrence parents feared for the lives of their children. The youngsters did not have proper clothing or shoes for frigid winter conditions, or enough food to keep them healthy. Haywood knew that people's concern for their children were of paramount importance. There

Without the meager wages the mills paid, parents could not feed their children. *(Library of Congress)*

was only one solution that would provide for the needs of the strikers' children and allow parents to continue to hold-out for better wages. Haywood had to get the children out of Lawrence.

Sending children away from their families during industrial strikes was a common strategy in European countries. The tactic had been successfully used in Italy, France, and Belgium. Knowing their children were fed and cared for eased parents' minds enough to allow them to continue to strike. In addition, public opinion usually shifted to support strikers when it became known that conditions were so dismal their children were forced to leave. Haywood called it a "war measure."

The exodus plan had never been attempted in the United States and could backfire if not handled with extreme care. The IWW placed an advertisement in a New York City newspaper asking for willing families to volunteer to adopt the strikers' children until the strike ended:

> Children of the Lawrence strikers are hungry. Their fathers and mothers are fighting against hunger, and hunger may break the strike. The men and women are willing to suffer, but they cannot watch their children's pain or hear their cries for food. Workers and strike sympathizers who can take a striker's child until the struggle ends are urged to send their name and address. . . . Do it at once.

Soon hundreds of phone calls and letters arrived in response to the request. Homes were promised for more than seven hundred children. Haywood arranged for two hundred to leave immediately.

Chapter 8

National Scandal

On February 10, 1912, nearly two hundred children gathered at the Franco-Belgian Hall to begin the cold walk to the Lawrence train station together. Mothers busily prepared sandwiches for the youngsters to eat on the train, or sat with their children at a long table, hastily filling out identification papers for the young travelers and organizing permission slips. Below the spaces for the children's names, ages, addresses, and nationalities were signature lines for parents to sign giving their permission for their children, ages two- to twelve-years-old, to leave the state of Massachusetts under the care of IWW representatives.

We, the undersigned, parents of the child above described, hereby agree that it is allowed to go to a vacation to people in _____ in care of the Lawrence strikers' committee, and we agree to allow the child to stay with the friend of the strikers in that city as long as the strike may last, except where unforeseen circumstances may make the return of the child necessary before the designated time.

    "Father_____
    "Mother_____
    "Custodian_____
    Approved by the strikers' committee.

The children's train was scheduled to leave at 8:20 a.m., bound first for Boston and then on to New York City. Most of the children had never been away from home; few had been away from their parents overnight.

William Haywood was responsible for the initial "war measure" strategy, but it was the added presence of Elizabeth Gurley Flynn that comforted worried parents that morning.

Flynn, though only twenty-one-years-old, was known as "The Rebel Girl" because of her powerful speeches and fervent belief in the rights of workers. She was an attractive woman and an engaging speaker who had a habit of leaning forward, over the podium, and throwing one arm into the air as she raised her voice to make her points. Intrigued with socialism as a young girl, Flynn had become a member of the IWW at the

Elizabeth Gurley Flynn speaking to strikers at a rally.

age of sixteen. Within a year of joining, she was one of its most promising strike organizers.

"When Elizabeth Gurley Flynn spoke," journalist Mary Heaton Vorse remembered, "the excitement of the crowd became a visible thing. She stood there, young, with her Irish blue eyes, her face magnolia white and her cloud of black hair, the picture of a youthful revolutionary girl leader. She stirred them, lifted them up in her appeal for solidarity."

Flynn's speeches drew large crowds in Lawrence and her enthusiasm re-energized weary strike participants. Mothers rallied around her, trusting The Rebel Girl to ensure the safety of their children.

Due to the confusion and excitement at the Franco-Belgian Hall, the families did not leave for the train station until 8:30 a.m. As the somber group traipsed over snowy sidewalks, some parents changed their minds and took their children home. The remaining travelers arrived at the depot minutes after the outbound train departed and arrangements were made for them to leave on the next one.

Not everyone who saw the strikers enter the station supported the mass exodus. An elderly man loudly informed the strikers that their youngsters should not be sent away because "good old Massachusetts can take care of her children."

A mother responded: "Sure, good old Massachusetts! Ha ha! Massachusetts send soldiers to shoot children's fathers. Massachusetts say to fathers, 'You work, work, all day you work.' Fathers say 'No more I work and children hungry.' Massachusetts say "Then we shoot!' Good old Massachusetts, ha ha!"

One hundred and nineteen children took seats on the next outbound train and, with Elizabeth Gurley Flynn and other

The station where the children left Lawrence to be taken care of by family and volunteers until the strike was over. *(Courtesy of Lawrence Public Library)*

IWW chaperones on board, they finally departed the station. A few of the younger children cried as they left, their faces pressed against the train's windows.

After a brief stop in Boston, the children continued on to New York's Grand Central Station, where they arrived just before 8:00 p.m. Five thousand New Yorkers welcome them with cheers, songs, and applause.

One by one, the Lawrence children stepped off the train and onto the crowded platform. They wore threadbare dresses or shirts and pants. Few had coats; none had luggage. All

Children on the train platform at Grand Central Station in New York
(Courtesy of Walter Reuther Library, Wayne State University)

were frightfully thin. In one large voice, they chanted words their IWW chaperones had taught them on the journey:

> Who are we? Who are we? Who are we?
> Yes we are! Yes we are! Yes we are!
> Strikers! Strikers! Strikers!

The greeting strangers hoisted the children onto their shoulders and carried them to the Labor Temple on the Upper East Side of New York City. By the time the tired and hungry youngsters were inside the building many were overwhelmed by the noisy attention and were in tears. The adults seated them at long tables and fed them hot soup, meat, rice, and potatoes. "Almost all snatched at their food with both fists and stuffed it down, they were so hungry," remembered Margaret Sanger, a nurse who accompanied them from Lawrence.

After the meal, each child was given a warm coat and examined by a doctor. Most of them were malnourished, one had chicken pox, one had diphtheria, and almost all had swollen tonsils. Many of the younger children fell asleep while waiting to be assigned to temporary families. It was late in the evening when they finally left the Labor Temple for homes.

Back in Lawrence, Mayor Scanlon did not celebrate. "I could scarcely believe that the strike leaders would do such a thing. . . . Lawrence could have very easily cared for these children."

While Flynn oversaw the children's exodus out of Lawrence, Ettor and Giovannitti were taken to court and formally charged with inciting the riot that led to Anna LoPizzo's death.

During the court proceedings, several witnesses came forward and gave testimony in support of the men's innocence. Fifteen-year-old Greta Zurwell, who had worked at the Everett Mill before the strike, reported that around five p.m. on the night of LoPizzo's death she left her home to determine why a large crowd had gathered on the streets outside.

"Did you see a woman on the ground?" an attorney asked her.

"Yes, right near me."

"Did you see her before she fell?"

"Yes."

"How many shots were fired?"

"Four or five."

"Did you see anyone fire the shots?"

"Yes."

"Who?"

"A policeman."

Zurwell pointed to Officer Oscar Benoit, who was sitting in the courtroom, and identified him as the man that had shot Anna LoPizzo. Several other witnesses also reported seeing a police officer fire the deadly shot, and some recognized Officer Benoit as the shooter. But the officer was not questioned and legal proceedings against Ettor and Giovannitti continued.

On Saturday, February 17, Elizabeth Gurley Flynn took an additional one hundred and fifty children out of the city by train. Some were sent to New York City and others were bound for Barre, Vermont to live with Italian families who worked in the granite quarries. Parents cried and waved handkerchiefs as the train pulled away from the station. The children nibbled on cookies given to them by their chaperones.

The New York-bound children were greeted by marching bands and thousands of well-wishers and marched in a parade down Fifth Avenue, carrying banners and signs proclaiming that they came from Lawrence seeking a home.

Margaret Sanger later described the children's physical appearance as emaciated and dejected. "Their garments were simply worn to shreds. Not a child had on any woolen clothing whatsoever, and only four wore overcoats. Never in all my nursing in the slums had I seen children in so ragged and deplorable a condition."

Lawrence city leaders and Massachusetts state officials were furious. Sending children away from home, they insisted, was anti-American and damaged community morale. Haywood and Flynn were accused of coercing parents into the extreme action, and of forcing some children to leave the city without parental consent. Colonel Sweetser informed the strikers that he would not permit any more children to leave unless they carried proof their parents were in full support of the departure.

Two days after the second group of children left, on Monday, February 19, two hundred police officers beat a group of women picketers with clubs. A Boston newspaper reporter described what he had seen: "Usually a night-stick well aimed brought the woman to the ground like a shot and instantly the police would be on her, pulling her in as many ways as there were police." U.S. Senator Miles Poindexter publicly rebuked the police for the unprecedented attack.

On Thursday, February 22, police officers prohibited a small group of children from going to Bridgeport, Connecticut when they arrived at the train station with their parents. "There will be no more children leav[ing] Lawrence," Marshal John J. Sullivan informed strikers. Sullivan had been promoted to the position of police chief only two days earlier because city officials thought his predecessor had not used firm enough measures against the strikers. "I will not hesitate," Sullivan assured his supporters, "to use all the force, power and authority I possess or may summon to my aid."

In spite of the new marshal's threat, strikers made plans to send an additional two hundred children to Philadelphia the following Saturday, February 24. Mayor Scanlon sent police officers into the tenements on the night of February 23 to warn parents against the plan. The next morning only forty-six children showed up at North Station. The adult chaperons carefully reviewed the papers authorizing them to accompany the children to Boston, and then on to sympathetic families in Philadelphia.

Children of the Lawrence strikers (*Library of Congress*)

As the children waited to board the train, Marshal Sullivan and fifty police officers entered the lobby. Sullivan loudly ordered the parents to take their children home. A few quietly left.

When the morning train chugged noisily into the station, the remaining mothers began organizing their boys and girls into a double line. Police blocked the doorway to the train platform. When a Polish woman, holding the hand of a small child, attempted to break through to the waiting train, police forced her back. This angered the gathered parents and suddenly the train station was chaotic. Men, women, children, and police officers began yelling, kicking, and punching. When it was over, several people were injured and many were arrested. The prisoners, including at least fifteen children, were taken to the local police station and locked inside jail cells to await preliminary hearings before the local judge.

"I saw the soldiers pick the children up by the legs like they were rags," remembered salesman Max Bogatin who was at the station that day, "and I saw one woman choked by a soldier."

That afternoon, Marshal Sullivan proudly told a newspaper reporter that the militia had not been needed to assist police with the morning's events. He noted that Lawrence police officers demonstrated "to the world that we are able to control the situation here without help."

Downstairs, as Sullivan was giving his self-congratulatory interview, a judge heard the cases of the arrested parents. He found them guilty of neglect because they had voluntarily attempted to send their children to live with strangers in cities hundreds of miles away. He also charged them with creating a disturbance.

With the charged parents and children lined up in front of him, the judge ordered the arrested children to be taken from their parents and placed in the City Home, a collection of three farmhouses located just outside Lawrence. The children were to be supervised by city employees until their parents were deemed fit to resume care for them.

As police attempted to gather the children together, mothers rushed forward. The police restrained the women and managed to get the children out of the courtroom. Outside, a crowd of five hundred people tried unsuccessfully to prevent the officers from loading the children into police vehicles.

U.S. senator William Borah *(left)* was among the senators who spoke out against the behavior of the Lawrence police.

The arrest of the children and their parents created even more tension in Lawrence. On Monday morning strikers marched, sang, threw bricks, and fired gunshots. Police broke up parades by swinging their clubs and firing their guns. Sixty-six people were arrested for a variety of crimes, ranging from obstruction of a public sidewalk to attempted murder.

As news of the beatings and arrests spread across the nation, Americans expressed shock over the behavior of the

Lawrence police department, especially the melee that had occurred at the city's train station. Even newspapers that had defended the mill owners began criticizing the tactics they were using to end the strike.

"The Lawrence authorities must be blind and the mill owners mad," claimed the *New York World*.

"All this occurred," reported the *Miami Herald*, "right here in America, almost within sight of the cradle of our boasted liberties."

Political leaders around the nation were drawn into the debate over the Lawrence textile strike. United States Senator William Borah said he could think of no authority of law that would keep parents from sending their children away from a dangerous environment. Cleveland Ohio's mayor predicted that America would not allow such warfare against labor to continue. An ex-speaker of the Massachusetts House of Representatives declared that the Lawrence police had "lost their heads."

Chapter 9
Congressional Hearing

The IWW took advantage of the public sentiment to promote its larger objectives. In a statement to the press, they redefined the battle between Lawrence's mill workers and its mill owners as a fight for far more than two hours worth of wages. Poor workers in Lawrence, the IWW proclaimed, were engaged in an epic struggle against the evil barons of American capitalism, who for years:

> have starved the workers and driven them to such an extent that their homes are homes no longer. Inasmuch as the mothers and children are driven by the low wages to work side by side with the father in the factory for a wage that spells bare existence and untimely death.
>
> We hold that as useful members of society, and as producers, we have the right to lead decent and honorable lives; that we are to have homes and not shacks; that we ought to have clean food and not adulterated food at high prices; that we ought to have clothes suited to the weather.

Letters and telegrams poured into the Congressional offices of state representatives in Washington, D.C. Some people demanded that Congress investigate the causes of the textile mill strike and the resulting violence at the Lawrence train station. Others demanded Congress do something to improve low factory wages. Many asked legislators to examine the actual business practices of textile mill owners, especially William Wood and his American Woolen Company.

Historically, the federal government had not interfered in relationships between individual states and industrial businesses. Since the beginning of the Industrial Revolution, the national government had preferred to let state governments solve their own business-related labor issues.

Socialist Congressman Victor Berger of Wisconsin viewed the events in Lawrence as proof that the federal government's hands-off attitude had failed to protect America's workers. He argued that when one state imposed laws designed to protect its laborers' rights, companies simply relocated to states with fewer restrictions. Berger proposed a Congressional investigation into the lives of the striking textile mill operators in Lawrence.

Representative William Wilson of Pennsylvania, chairman of the House Committee on Labor, supported the initiative, noting that there had been, "many conflicts between capital and labor" in the United States in recent decades. "But as far as I know, there has never occurred in the history of trade disputes in this country any conditions approaching or even approximating the conditions which are alleged to exist at Lawrence, Massachusetts."

Other congressmen were hesitant to act. They insisted it was not the role of the federal government to make decisions affecting individual states' economic concerns. Berger compromised by suggesting a hearing into two Lawrence issues which clearly fell under federal jurisdiction. First, Congress would determine if any individual's constitutional rights were violated at the Lawrence train station on February 24, 1912. Second, Congress would determine if any interstate commerce laws were broken when ticket-holding passengers were prohibited from leaving Massachusetts by train.

Congressional leaders accepted the more limited investigation and a hearing was scheduled. A telegram went out to IWW union leader William Haywood asking him to send strikers to Washington, D.C., to answer questions.

On Friday, March 1, a thousand people gathered at the Lawrence train station to cheer the departure of thirteen adolescent strikers and several adults bound for the nation's capital. A few of the children carried small bundles wrapped in newspapers, containing clothes to sleep in and combs. None had suitcases. Before they left, the crowd gave three cheers for the United States Constitution and then three cheers for the American working class.

Later that day, Mayor Scanlon announced that Lawrence mill owners were now willing to raise workers' wages by 5 percent. To receive the extra pay, the mayor added, workers would have to end the strike and return to their jobs no later than March 6. The offer was issued directly to the workers, with no mention of the IWW labor union. The mill owners were still refusing to recognize the union.

Most workers had lost more than twenty-two cents per week in wages when the state's new law dropped the maximum workweek from fifty-six hours to fifty-four. The 5 percent "raise" meant a reinstatement of less than a nickel for

House Office Building in Washington, D.C. *(Library of Congress)*

most of them. Haywood announced the offer to the strikers, but reminded them that the small increase "would not yield pennies enough to cover the eyes of babies that have died as a result of the strike." The strike committee voted unanimously to reject the offer and reiterated in their statement that the Lawrence Strike of 1912 would continue until all demands were met and Ettor and Giovannitti were released from jail.

On Saturday morning, March 2, at the House Office Building near the Capitol in Washington, D.C., a panel of congressmen, all members of the House Committee on Rules, sat behind long tables in a huge room surrounded by marble-lined walls and long curtained windows. Most likely, many of the suits worn by the legislators came from fabric produced by American Woolen Company. The Lawrence textile mill strikers sat facing them; onlookers and aides filled remaining seats.

After a few remarks detailing the purpose of the hearing, Congressman Berger pointed to the small contingent of Lawrence strikers and told the congressmen, "I have here from Lawrence some of the workers employed [by AWC] and I propose to let them tell their own story."

The first person to testify was Samuel Lipson. Twenty-nine-years-old, Lipson had worked as a weaver at Wood Worsted Mill for three years, and had participated in the IWW's attempt to send children out of Lawrence on February 24.

> "Why did you go on a strike?" Berger asked him.
> "I went out on a strike," Lipson replied, "because I was unable to make a living for my family."
> "How many children do you have?"
> "I have four children and a wife."
> "Did you have steady work?"
> "Usually the work was steady, but there was times when I used to make from $3 to $4 and $5 per week. We have had to live on $3 per week. We lived on bread and water."
> "How much were you reduced by reason of the recent cut in the wages?" Berger asked.
> "From 50 to 65 to 75 cents per week," Lipson answered.
> "How much does a loaf of bread cost in Lawrence?"
> "Twelve cents; that is what I pay."
> "The reduction in your wages, according to this, took away five loaves of bread from you every week?"
> "Yes, sir. When we go into the store now with a dollar and get a peck of potatoes and a few other things, we have no change left out of that dollar. Of course we are living according to what we get."

"How many of the workers of Lawrence are women and children?" Berger asked.

"I can not tell you about how many, but I can tell you that the majority of them are women and children. . . . These children are doing more work. If they can not do the work, they are fired out. They must do the work that goes from one machine to another. . . . If they do not speed up, they are fired out."

"What are the demands of the strikers now?" Berger asked.

"The demands are 15 percent increase in wages, based on 54 hours per week and double pay for overtime. These people," Lipton said, pointing to other strikers in the room, "work sometimes only two or three days in a week. Her father works only three days in a week, and has $2.88 per week for the family, and they absolutely live on bread and water. If you would look at the other children, you would see that they look like skeletons."

Berger asked: "Mr. Lipson, will you tell me what was the reason the strikers sent their children away?"

Young textile workers

> "I sent my child away because I did not want my child to
> see what is going on in that city. He said to me, 'Why did the
> soldiers try to hurt those people and put the bayonets against
> them?'"
> "Where did you send your child?"
> "To New York."
> "Your child is well taken care of?"
> "He is well taken care of."
> "How old is the little fellow?"
> "He is 8 years old."

Berger asked Lipson if it made it easier for the strikers
to continue to strike without their young children waiting
at home.

> "Why certainly," Lipson said, "we know well that when the
> child is between the parents and the mill owner we will be
> compelled to go [back to work in] the mill when we hear the
> cry from the child, 'Give me something to eat.'"
> "So," said Berger, "it is simply that the mill owners gain by
> keeping the children in Lawrence. They break the strike this
> way?"
> "Certainly."

Berger then questioned Lipson about specific events at
the Lawrence train station on February 24. Did police show
him any papers which said he legally could not send children out of Lawrence?

No, nothing at all.

Had tickets been purchased for the children's departure?

Yes, at least forty for the children and ten for the adults
that would chaperon them.

Was that the total number of children scheduled to leave
that day?

No. One hundred were supposed to leave, but only forty got there before police and militia arrived.

Only forty of them could get in the depot due to military and police interference?

Yes.

Representative Edward Pou of North Carolina asked Lipson to describe how police prevented children from boarding the train.

> "It happened like this," Lipson said. "I took charge of the children and told the children to be ready and we will march out and board the train. . . . As soon as the children started to go out . . . [the police] tried to grab one child from the mother and to grab the woman, and so on, trying to arrest the children right off, and trying to get hold of the mothers and pull them and push them and club them, and doing all kinds of things. They had . . . a patrol wagon and a big ambulance to arrest them and carry them away."
>
> "Just a moment," Congressman Pou interrupted, "Did you see any mother of any child clubbed there by a policeman?"
>
> "I saw the policemen with their clubs club a woman, while putting them into the wagons, in the breast and stomach and all that, and grab them by the hair and so on, you know. I saw it."
>
> "Did they prevent any children from boarding the train?" Congressman Pou continued.
>
> "Certainly. They gave no chance at all. They grabbed hold of the children and they put them into that big patrol wagon. In fact, one policeman took a child and threw her into the wagon, and she got a black eye."
>
> "How old was the child?"
>
> "Seven years old."

The Lawrence children were scheduled to testify on Monday, and Congress recessed for the remainder of the weekend. On

Child workers from Lawrence were sent to Washington to testify before Congress. William Haywood stands in the back, second from the left. *(Courtesy of Walter Reuther Library, Wayne State University)*

Sunday, the children toured the nation's capital city and met with President William Howard Taft. The president was so moved by their impoverished appearance that, after shaking each child's hand, he gave their chaperones a check for one thousand dollars of his own personal money.

On Monday morning, people filed into the stately room on Capital Hill once again and testimony resumed. One by one the thirteen Lawrence children were asked questions

President William Howard Taft *(Library of Congress)*

about their lives and their work in the textile city. Initially, the naive congressmen questioned the children as they might have queried their own, asking light-hearted questions related to play and opportunities for learning.

> Do you read books?
> I don't have much time.
> Do you like to play?
> Sure, sometimes on Sunday.
> Do you like school?

I had to quit to work in the mill.
Did you like school?
Yes.
What kind of food do you eat at home?
Bread and water.

It did not take long for the congressional leaders to realize they were not interviewing young people who had the chance to enjoy their childhoods. The Lawrence children were only fourteen or fifteen-years-old, but they knew much more about hardships of industrial work and poverty than they did about baseball or tag. Most of them had quit school when they were fourteen; a few had started work illegally at younger ages. They earned between $5.10 and $6.55 per

Many children in Lawrence quit school by age fourteen to work in the mills. *(Library of Congress)*

week when the mills were in full operation during winter months. They earned as low as $2 or $3 a week during summers' more limited production schedules. All of them reported giving their paychecks to their parents in order to support their families.

One child who captured Congress' full attention was a girl named Camella Teoli. Camella's testimony was dramatic because of her age and because of an injury she suffered while working in a Lawrence mill. At the end of one work shift, Camella released her long hair from its tight bun at the back of her head and let it fall over her shoulders. Someone called her name, and as she spun around to see who it was, her hair got caught in the draft gear of a spinning frame. The hair, and the skin it was attached to, were yanked from her scalp. Other employees rushed forward to stop the machine and someone quickly wrapped the pieces of her scalp in a newspaper. Camella was rushed to a hospital where doctors stitched the scalp back to her head.

> CHAIRMAN WILSON: Camella, how old are you?
> CAMELLA: Fourteen years and eight months.
> CHAIRMAN: Fourteen years and eight months?
> CAMELLA: Yes.
> CHAIRMAN: How many children are there in your family?
> CAMELLA: Five.
> CHAIRMAN: Where do you work?
> CAMELLA: In the woolen mill.
> CHAIRMAN: For the American Woolen Co.?
> CAMELLA: Yes.
> CHAIRMAN: What sort of work do you do?
> CAMELLA: Twisting.
> CHAIRMAN: You do twisting?
> CAMELLA: Yes.
> CHAIRMAN: How much do you get a week?

CAMELLA: $6.55.

CHAIRMAN: What is the smallest pay?

CAMELLA: $2.64.

CHAIRMAN: Do you have to pay anything for water?

CAMELLA: Yes.

CHAIRMAN: How much?

CAMELLA: Ten cents every two weeks.

CHAIRMAN: Now, did you ever get hurt in the mill?

CAMELLA: Yes.

CHAIRMAN: Can you tell the committee about that—how it happened and what it was?

CAMELLA: Yes.

CHAIRMAN: Tell us about it now, in your own way.

CAMELLA: Well, I used to go to school, and then a man came up to my house and asked my father why I didn't go to work, so my father says I don't know whether she is 13 or 14 years old. So, the man say you give me $4 and I will make the papers come from the old country saying you are 14. So, my father gave him the $4, and in one month came the papers that I was 14. I went to work, and [after] about two weeks got hurt in my head.

CHAIRMAN: Now, how did you get hurt, and where were you hurt in the head; explain that to the committee?

CAMELLA: I got hurt in Washington.

CHAIRMAN: In the Washington Mill?

CAMELLA: Yes, sir.

CHAIRMAN: What part of your head?

CAMELLA: My head.

CHAIRMAN: Well, how were you hurt?

CAMELLA: The machine pulled the scalp off.

CHAIRMAN: The machine pulled your scalp off?

CAMELLA: Yes, sir.

CHAIRMAN: How long ago was that?

CAMELLA: A year ago, or about a year ago.

CHAIRMAN: Were you in the hospital after that?

CAMELLA: I was in the hospital seven months.

CHAIRMAN: Seven months?

CAMELLA: Yes.

CHAIRMAN: Are you working now?

CAMELLA: Yes, sir.

CHAIRMAN: How much are you getting?

CAMELLA: $6.55.

CHAIRMAN: Are you working in the same place where you were before you were hurt?

CAMELLA: No.

CHAIRMAN: How long did you go to school?

CAMELLA: I left when I was in the sixth grade.

CHAIRMAN: You left when you were in the sixth grade?

CAMELLA: Yes, sir.

REP. THOMAS HARDWICK OF GEORGIA: Are you one of the strikers?

CAMELLA: Yes, sir.

REP. HARDWICK: Did you agree to the strike before it was ordered; did they ask you anything about striking before you quit?

CAMELLA: No.

REP. HARDWICK: But you joined them after they quit?

CAMELLA: Yes.

REP. HARDWICK: Why did you do that?

CAMELLA: Because I didn't get enough to eat at home.

Moved by Camella's account, the congressmen no longer insisted on limiting the scope of the hearing to abstract questions of constitutional rights and interstate commerce laws. Instead, the legislators wanted to further investigate the strike's rationale and try to understand why it had gone on so long.

Margaret Sanger, a trained nurse who accompanied many strikers' children to New York, testified that the families that took the children into their homes were shocked by their thin clothing. Only a few of the children had worn anything under their threadbare dresses or shirts to keep them warm in the brutally cold temperatures that plagued the northeast that winter.

Margaret Sanger *(Library of Congress)*

"You stated this morning," Chairman Wilson reminded Miss Sanger, "that four of the children out of the one hundred and nineteen had on underclothing. It was suggested during the noon hour by individuals to me that the rest of the children were possibly in the habit of wearing underclothing during the cold weather, but that it had been taken off to create a little more sympathy, or excite a little more sympathy. Do you know whether or not these children were in the habit of wearing underclothing?"

"Some of the fathers and mothers," Miss Sanger replied, "brought them to the station with their own clothing wrapped around them to keep them from the cold."

"Do you think," Chairman Wilson insisted, "that these same children, when going to New York, wore their poorest clothing, thinking that they would be replenished when they got in New York by your friends, and that they left their better clothing at home for the purpose of getting more out of it than if they had taken their other clothing?"

"I thought of that at the time," Miss Sanger confessed, "and I asked the children if they had any better clothing, and not one of them had. They wore the best clothing they had. They all tried to look their very best. The girls wore their best ribbons."

After Sanger's testimony, the congressmen questioned representatives from Lawrence's police department, its local businesses, mill paymasters, and religious leaders. All denied the existence of slums in Lawrence and claimed the workers had adequate housing and food, and sufficient clothing.

Marshal John J. Sullivan was asked about the violence at the Lawrence train station. He testified there was no violence on the part of his police officers. What about reports of an officer beating a woman with a club, one congressman queried. The officer, Sullivan replied, was merely attempting to keep the woman from falling off the truck. How did that explain the reports of brutality reported in almost all of the newspapers? Newspaper reporters, Sullivan said, sensationalized the story to sell their papers.

Representative Augustus Stanley of Kentucky pointed out to Sullivan the dismal physical condition of the strikers' children.

"I have seen worse clad people on the streets of Washington since I have been here," Sullivan replied.

"Yes," the congressman remarked, "but you never saw them arrested while trying peacefully to board a train."

Reverend Clark Carter, a prominent Congregational minister who had lived in Lawrence for twenty-five years, testified that the strike parades were mob activities and blamed any poverty, which he called "narrow circumstances," on the individual shortcomings of immigrant workers. He told Congress that the strikers' children were sent to New York without proper clothing in order to gain sympathy for the strike. He informed them that bread and molasses were proof of the abundance available to Lawrence workers since there were other places in the world where people had to eat bread without molasses.

When asked about the wisdom of young children working in mills, Reverend Carter replied he saw nothing wrong with children quitting school and entering the workforce. Mill work, he testified, was a better education. "Those that are idle until they are sixteen years of age do not amount to much afterwards."

As testimony concluded in Washington, D.C., forty-two children left Lawrence to live with families in Philadelphia. Also, William Wood learned that his company profits for the prior year's recording period were nearly $11.6 million. Congress resolved to launch a full-scale investigation into William Wood and his lucrative textile empire.

Chapter 10

The End of the Strike

A federal investigation into the textile mill industry was not something William Wood wanted to happen. His wool empire enjoyed protection from foreign competition because of steep tariffs the federal government levied on imported woolen goods. He feared that an investigation could lead to an end of the tariffs, which would lead to increased competition from foreign producers and force AWC to lower its prices. The best thing he could hope for from a federal investigation was months of inconvenience as investigators poured over his books, interviewed his managers and employees, and questioned his business practices.

Suddenly, William Wood was motivated to end the Lawrence strike.

On Thursday March 7, as the strikers who had testified before Congress returned to Lawrence, William Wood and several mill owners broke their vow to not negotiate and met with the strikers' Committee of Ten at the State House in

Boston. The meeting lasted all day. When it ended, Wood promised to raise worker wages if strikers returned to their jobs immediately.

The Committee of Ten demanded to know exactly how much each worker would receive when they returned to work. Wood told the Committee exact figures would take two weeks to calculate. He wanted the strikers to return to work while the numbers were being determined but the Committee refused.

Wood then offered to provide exact financial numbers within a few days if workers would return to work immediately. The Committee refused to discuss any resumption of work until the exact wage numbers were provided.

Two days later, a Saturday, mill owners sent representatives to meet with the Committee of Ten again. The representatives presented a breakdown of proposed wage raises, categorized by mill departments. The Committee wanted exact details of wages based on specific mill jobs, the Committee insisted, not vague estimates based on groups of workers. They refused to go back to work. The mill agents left, pledging to contact the Committee again by Monday with more precise figures.

The numerous meetings between mill agents and strikers made Mayor Scanlon optimistic that the strike was coming to an end. He allowed some militia troops to leave Lawrence. The strikers were less optimistic. They sent fifteen more children to live with families in Manchester, New Hampshire.

William Haywood spent the weekend in New York giving speeches to encourage textile workers there to follow the lead of the strikers in Lawrence. He warned other New England mill owners and investors to pay attention to events

Strike parade *(Courtesy of Walter Reuther Library, Wayne State University)*

in the Massachusetts city, predicting that once its strike was settled, workers in other parts of the region would demand better pay, too.

Mill owners in the states of Maine, New Hampshire, and Rhode Island heeded Haywood's advice and began discussing wage increases for their employees. Mill cities in which raises where not forthcoming, such as Lowell and Fall River, Massachusetts, would soon experience copycat strikes, just as Haywood predicted.

When the work week started on the morning of Monday, March 11, 10,000 strikers marched in a picket line that extended several city blocks. They shouted at police and sang songs. Some wore IWW buttons; others carried pictures of the imprisoned Ettor and Giovannitti.

Meanwhile, the Committee of Ten waited to be contacted by mill representatives from Boston. The call did not come until Tuesday afternoon.

When the Committee arrived at the State House to receive specific details regarding pay increases for Lawrence workers, William Wood and his managers from AWC were present. The meeting lasted several hours; when it ended, the Committee of Ten had William Wood's best offer in front of them.

Every textile worker at AWC, according to Wood's new proposal, would receive a raise in hourly pay, but it would not be the straightforward 15 percent increase the IWW had demanded. Instead, Wood offered to pay workers varying increases in wages. Those who made the most money before the strike would receive 5 percent increases in weekly pay; those making the least would receive 20 percent increases. Workers in between the two extremes would get raises between 5 and 20 percent, depending on their rates of pay prior to the strike.

Wood also agreed to pay time and quarter to each worker for overtime work, to modify the bonus system, and to ensure no discrimination would be shown to anyone who had participated in the strike. No agreement was reached regarding the imprisonment of Ettor and Giovannitti. Wood said it was a matter of the state courts and out of his control, although the workers knew he could use his influence and have the two men released.

It was raining on Wednesday morning when strikers packed into the Franco-Belgian Hall at 10:00 a.m. to hear the report of the Committee's meeting with William Wood. Haywood called the meeting to order and then revealed the terms of the negotiated agreement.

Excitement spread through the crowded room as terms were disclosed. Haywood cautioned that the agreement was limited to workers at William Wood's AWC, but he expected other mills to make similar offers. A vote would be necessary before the agreement could be officially accepted or declined. It would be taken on the Lawrence common the following afternoon.

"You, the strikers of Lawrence," Haywood said, "have won the most signal victory of any body of organized working men in the world. You have won in face of the armed forces. . . . You have won the struggle by your splendid solidarity."

The crowd responded with a roaring cheer followed by clapping, dancing and singing. After nine and a half weeks, the grueling Lawrence textile mill strike was nearing an end. Victory belonged to the strikers!

On the afternoon of March 14, 1912, sixty-three days

Elizabeth Gurley Flynn *(center)* and William Haywood *(far right)* arrived in Lawrence to poll the strikers about ending the strike.

after the violent textile strike had started, more than 15,000 workers, representing twenty-five different countries, and speaking close to four dozen languages, gathered at the city park in Lawrence. Some talked and others sang familiar strike songs as they waited for Big Bill Haywood to arrive.

When Haywood and Elizabeth Gurley Flynn finally wove their way through the assembled crowd, a loud cheer rang out. Haywood hopped up to the podium and, as soon as the applause quieted, informed the anxious textile operatives that their strike committee had a report to make.

One by one representatives from each participating nationality read the terms of the agreement in his or her native language. Haywood then informed the strikers that the terms of the agreement had been accepted by the American Woolen Company, the Kunhardt Mill, and the Atlantic Mill. He said the strike would continue against the other mills until they agreed to meet with the strike committee.

He had to shout to be heard by everyone on the common, but when Haywood asked the strikers if they were willing to accept the terms of the agreement, 15,000 hands immediately shot into the air. When he asked if anyone was opposed to the terms, only six hands were raised. The strikers agreed to return to work the following Monday.

Within ten days of the initial, jubilant vote, the remaining mills in Lawrence agreed to terms similar to those established with William Wood. The strike committee held its final meeting on March 24 and voted itself out of existence. Haywood and Flynn left Lawrence to organize the copycat strikes that were taking hold in other textile mills around New England. In the days and weeks that followed, a sense of normalcy returned to Lawrence, Massachusetts.

CHILDREN OF THE STRIKERS RETURN

Made Grand Central Station in New York Resound With Strains of "Star Spangled Banner"---All in Good Health---Bearing Flowers to Loved Ones---Grand Reception and Parade in This City.

New York, March 30—The stirring strains of the "Star Spangled Banner" swept through the Grand Central station as thousands of commuters emerged from the trains at 8 o'clock this morning. The singers were 240 children of the strikers with happy and contented faces scrubbed to a picturesquely healthy glow, returning from the homes of refuge here and in Philadelphia to their parents at Lawrence.

LAWRENCE RECOVERING FROM THE STRIKE

The Tribune stated a few days ago that Lawrence could make a

Newspaper headlines herald the return of the children.

With the strike over, the Congressional House Rules Committee in Washington, D.C., canceled all pending investigations into the textile industry. William Wood was once again free to focus on increasing his company's value without immediate fear of federal intervention.

On March 30, the children who had been sent away from Lawrence began returning home. Most had gained weight and all wore new clothes purchased by their temporary families. Some carried toys or flowers and many wore badges demanding the release of Ettor and Giovannitti. The youngsters were paraded through town on horse-drawn wagons

123

as people lined the streets, or hung out of open windows, to wave at them.

Residents of Lawrence could finally think about more than meetings, unions, and strike strategies. The United States had added two new states while they battled for better wages: New Mexico was admitted on January 6 and Arizona on February 14. They joined the rest of the nation in mourning the loss of more than 1,500 lives when the world's largest ship, the Titanic, which had been advertised as unsinkable, hit an iceberg during its maiden voyage in April and sank into the Atlantic Ocean. They also wondered if there was any credibility to the rumor that Massachusetts' state government was planning to pass a minimum-wage law that summer.

RMS *Titanic (Library of Congress)*

The only strike-related issue that continued to plague Lawrence for the remainder of the year was the imprisonment of Ettor and Giovannitti. The two strike leaders languished in jail, without the ability to post bail, as they had since their arrest in January.

A third man, twenty-seven-year-old mill worker Joseph Caruso, was also held in connection with the death of Anna LoPizzo. Initially, Caruso was arrested for assaulting a police officer with a knife during the riot on the night of January 29. But when several prominent Massachusetts lawyers argued that the city could not continue to hold Ettor and Giovannitti as accessories to murder if no one had been arrested for the actual murder, Caruso was charged with assisting an unknown mystery man in LoPizzo's shooting. He denied any involvement in her death.

The imprisonment of the three men, especially Ettor and Giovannitti, enraged mill workers around New England and elicited sympathy from laborers around the world. Industrial employees staged huge protest marches and rallies in Germany, South Africa, and Australia. American products were boycotted by workers in Sweden and Italy. Supportive laborers from around the globe donated nearly $60,000 to the IWW for use in the men's defense.

Union organizations across the United States also took an interest in the outcome of Ettor and Giovannitti's trial. If the two men, as IWW leaders, were found to be personally responsible for violence others had committed during the Lawrence strike—simply because of words they had spoken—it would have serious repercussions for all future labor strikes. Union leaders would live in constant fear of imprisonment for any crime that was committed during a strike.

After a series of court hearings over the summer, Ettor and Giovannitti's trial date was set for late September. All three defendants were scheduled to face a jury at the same time: Caruso for helping an unknown man to commit murder; Ettor and Giovannitti for being accessories to the act. The punishment for each man, if found guilty, was death.

As the trial date approached, Massachusetts officials feared passionate protests would erupt throughout the state in support of the popular prisoners. In anticipation of trouble, state authorities announced they would arrest any IWW representatives who attempted to rally crowds within Massachusetts' borders. Lawrence city officials made it known that they intended to indict William Haywood and other union agitators for conspiracy to incite violence and intimidation.

Haywood stayed out of Lawrence to avoid arrest, but did give a speech in Boston on September 15 to an audience of more than 17,000 people, many of them Lawrence mill workers who had journeyed to the city by train to hear him speak. As state officials had feared, Haywood asked his listeners if they were willing to stage another massive strike against Massachusetts' employers to gain the release of Ettor and Giovannitti. The responding cheers could be heard several blocks away.

After the rousing speech, police arrested Haywood and took him to jail, where he was held on twenty-two counts of conspiracy. Haywood claimed he was "guilty of nothing except trying to help the workers of Lawrence get a little more bread."

As rumors of a new strike circulated, Ettor and Giovannitti sent letters from jail asking supporters not to stage a sympathy strike on their behalf. A sudden strike, they feared, would

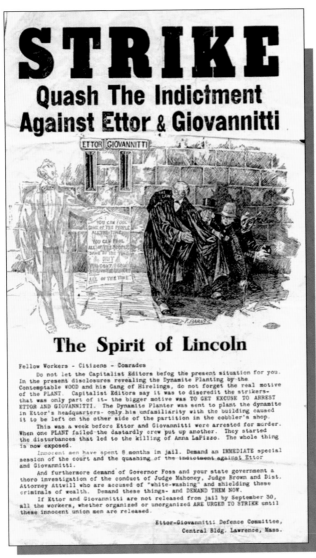

STRIKE
Quash The Indictment
Against Ettor & Giovannitti

ETTOR GIOVANNITTI

The Spirit of Lincoln

Fellow Workers - Citizens - Comrades

Do not let the Capitalist Editors befog the present situation for you. In the present disclosures revealing the Dynamite Planting by the Contemptable WOOD and his Gang of Hirelings, do not forget the real motive of the PLANT. Capitalist Editors say it was to discredit the strikers- that was only part of it- the bigger motive was TO GET EXCUSE TO ARREST ETTOR AND GIOVANNITTI. The Dynamite Planter was sent to plant the dynamite in Ettor's headquarters- only his unfamiliarity with the building caused it to be left on the other side of the partition in the cobbler's shop.

This was a week before Ettor and Giovannitti were arrested for murder. When one PLANT failed-the dastardly crew put up another. They started the disturbances that led to the killing of Anna LaPizzo. The whole thing is now exposed.

Innocent men have spent 8 months in jail. Demand an IMMEDIATE special session of the court and the quashing of the indictment against Ettor and Giovannitti.

And furthermore demand of Governor Foss and your state government a thero investigation of the conduct of Judge Mahoney, Judge Brown and Dist. Attorney Attwill who are accused of "white-washing" and shielding these criminals of wealth. Demand these things- and DEMAND THEM NOW.

If Ettor and Giovannitti are not released from jail by September 30, all the workers, whether organized or unorganized ARE URGED TO STRIKE until these innocent union men are released.

Ettor-Giovannitti Defence Committee,
Central Bldg. Lawrence, Mass.

A flyer passed out to workers in support of Ettor and Giovannitti

turn public opinion against them and jeopardize their ability to get a fair trial. But on Friday, September 27, 12,000 workers walked off their jobs in a brief protest of their imprisonment. The Wood, Ayer, Everett, Arlington, and Pacific mills in Lawrence were forced to temporarily suspend operations.

One reporter labeled the strikers' action as "The Second Battle of Lawrence."

On September 30, three hundred and fifty men were summoned to the courthouse in Salem, Massachusetts to be questioned as potential jurors. The three prisoners were brought to the courthouse, led inside, and locked in an iron cage in the center of the courtroom to witness the jury selection proceedings.

Expecting the trial to last several months, almost all of the potential jurors offered excuses for why they could not serve. More men had to be called to the courthouse for questioning before a jury of twelve could be selected. The fate of Ettor, Giovannitti and Caruso was to be decided by four carpenters, two leather workers, a sailmaker, a grocer, a driver, a lamp maker, a stock fitter, and a hairdresser.

Salem courthouse *(Library of Congress)*

Once the trial commenced, Ettor, Giovannitti and Caruso were delivered to the courthouse each day from a Salem jail and were locked inside the iron cage to hear testimony. Lawyers for the prosecution and defense asked jurors to think about the men's guilt or innocence as each witness testified before the court. Did Joseph Caruso somehow assist another, unknown man in the killing of Anna LoPizzo? If he did, did he do it because of words he heard spoken by Joseph Ettor and Arturo Giovannitti? Did words in speeches make Ettor and Giovannitti partners in LoPizzo's murder?

The final question had a powerful legal precedent that the prosecutors hoped would lead to a conviction. In 1887, a bomb was thrown into a crowd during a labor protest at Haymarket Square in Chicago. Seven people were eventually sentenced to death by an Illinois court for the explosion. None of the seven was accused of actually throwing the bomb, but all had written incendiary words in journals that the prosecution and police argued had prompted the attack.

In October 1912, as the Boston Red Sox baseball team celebrated its World Series win over the New York Giants, the prosecution in the Ettor-Giovannitti trial, as it was commonly called, grilled more than seventy witnesses about events in Lawrence leading up to Anna LoPizzo's death. Some people recalled seeing Joseph Caruso at the scene. A few repeated violent words they remembered Ettor and Giovannitti saying. Someone testified that Ettor ordered strikers to buy guns, and someone else remembered Giovannitti encouraging them to take violent action.

In November 1912, as Democrat Woodrow Wilson celebrated his election as President of the United States over

Republican incumbent William Howard Taft and third-party candidate and former president Theodore Roosevelt, the defense team presented its case. Witnesses came forward to testify they had seen a police officer fire the shot that killed Anna LoPizzo, not Joseph Caruso. Caruso's wife testified that her husband was at home eating dinner when the shooting occurred. Numerous people insisted that speeches of Ettor and Giovannitti had consistently encouraged strikers to remain nonviolent.

For weeks, jurors patiently listened as prosecution and defense witnesses discussed details of the strike. They learned about the impact of Ettor's first speech at city hall and listened to descriptions of the attack on city streetcars. They guessed at meanings behind the strike leaders' speeches, carefully considering each word and phrase.

Finally, Ettor and Giovannitti were asked to testify in their own defense. Each man talked for several hours about specific words he had chosen to use in his speeches and defended his actions and intentions during the strike. Each encouraged the jury to deliver a verdict of innocence. Then, without fanfare, the fate of Ettor, Giovannitti, and Caruso was placed in the hands of twelve men.

On Saturday, November 23, three days before the jury gave its long-awaited verdict, Ettor and Giovannitti requested permission to speak to the court once more. Knowing that their lives depended on the jury's forthcoming decision, Ettor spoke first.

"I have not been tried on my acts," he said. "I have been tried here because of my social ideas. Does [the District Attorney] believe . . . that the cross or the gallows or the guillotine . . . ever settled an idea? It never did. If an idea can live, it lives because history adjudges it right. And what has been considered an idea constituting a social crime in one age has in the next age become the religion of humanity."

Giovannitti asked the jurors to think beyond strike strategies and union methods in their judgment of his guilt or innocence. He told them that he and Joseph Ettor were not to blame for the terrible relationship which led to a strike between Lawrence's mill owners and its mill workers. He said it was the industrial system that had caused so much unrest and upheaval in the city. He asked jurors to consider the morality of industrial America itself. "What about the better and nobler humanity where there shall be no more slaves, where no man will ever be obliged to go on strike in order to obtain fifty cents a week more, where children will not have to starve any more." He vowed that if allowed to go free, he and Ettor would continue to speak out until the rights of American workers were guaranteed.

Two days before Thanksgiving Day, and two months after the start of the trial, a large crowd assembled at the Salem courthouse to hear the jury's judgment. Ettor, Giovannitti, and Caruso arrived, each wearing a red carnation on his suit jacket and smiling as he was locked into the cage in the center of the courtroom. The jury delivered its verdict: Joseph Ettor, Arturo Giovannitti, and Joseph Caruso were found not guilty.

Cheers erupted in the courtroom as the three men were released from the iron cage and embraced by the joyful crowd. Ettor thanked the jury on behalf of the "working class." Giovannitti thanked them "in the name of justice, truth, and civilization." Caruso, through an Italian interpreter, simply thanked the jury and said "he didn't do it."

Chapter 11
Immigrant City

On Thanksgiving Day 1912, Joseph Ettor gave his final speech in Lawrence to the city's textile mill workers. He told them that the United States owed thanks to its working class. The country, he said, should be grateful its workers went hungry so mill bosses could eat. He encouraged his listeners to continue to rebel against American capitalism, reminding them that they did not need guns or dynamite to gain better pay or greater respect in the workplace. Laborers, Ettor said, had the ultimate weapon against those that imprisoned them in a wage system: if they stopped working, the capitalist class would starve.

In the months following his final Lawrence speech, Ettor resumed his role as an IWW leader. He organized other strikes around the country. His last official visit to Lawrence was in 1916 at the invitation of workers from the Pacific Mill who planned another strike. Shortly after Ettor arrived, however, Lawrence police broke into his room at the Needham Hotel, took him to the city's train station, and forced him to leave town. Ettor accused the police of kidnapping and assault, but a local judge dismissed his case.

Later that year, Ettor and William Haywood had a disagreement regarding decisions made in Minnesota's Iron Range Strike, which resulted in Ettor's resignation from the IWW. Ettor spent the rest of his life in California, operating a wine-making business and writing articles in support of workers' rights. He died in 1948.

Arturo Giovannitti continued to participate in IWW-led strikes and labor rallies until a paralysis in his legs caused him to quit. Throughout his life, Giovannitti wrote and published poetry that raged against cruelty and poverty in American society. He died at home in New York in 1959.

Elizabeth Gurley Flynn left the IWW the same time Ettor did, but continued to work against the injustices she thought were inherent in the American industrial system. In the 1930s, she joined the Communist Party and became a party leader. In 1952, she was charged with supporting the overthrow of the United States' government; after a nine-month long trial, she was found guilty and served a two-year prison sentence. Upon her release Flynn left the United States. She died in Moscow in 1964.

Patriotism consumed the nation when the United States entered World War I in 1917, and "Big Bill" Haywood's outspoken demands for changes to the American economic system were viewed as unpatriotic. The federal government arrested Haywood, along with more than one hundred IWW supporters, for organizing strikes during wartime. Charged with violating espionage and sedition acts, they were all convicted. Haywood filed an appeal and was released from prison

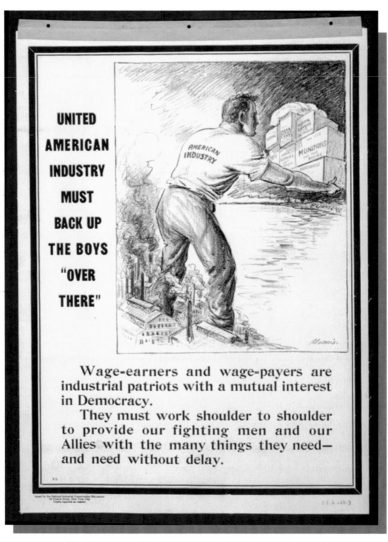

UNITED AMERICAN INDUSTRY MUST BACK UP THE BOYS "OVER THERE"

Wage-earners and wage-payers are industrial patriots with a mutual interest in Democracy.
They must work shoulder to shoulder to provide our fighting men and our Allies with the many things they need— and need without delay.

Poster supporting World War I *(Library of Congress)*

to await a new hearing. When the Supreme Court rejected his final appeal in 1921, Haywood used a false passport to escape the United States. He died in Moscow in 1928.

The Industrial Workers of the World remained an active labor union, but internal leadership struggles and governmental persecution took its toll and membership declined

IWW members in New York *(Library of Congress)*

following World War I. Almost one hundred years after The Lawrence Strike of 1912, the IWW still exists and continues to welcome all wage earners into its union. It still promotes its vision of a world in which wages and profits do not exist and toward a global economic system in which workers are entitled to everything they produce.

Finally, of all the major participants in the Lawrence Strike, William Wood's life took perhaps the most intriguing course. After the strike ended, a man named Ernest Pitman of Lawrence confessed he had been the one to obtain the dynamite that John Breen had planted throughout the city in January 1912. Pitman implicated several prominent mill owners in the plot. The words "approved-William M. Wood, president" appeared at the bottom of American Woolen

Company vouchers that had been used to pay the implicated men. Shortly after Pitman came forward, authorities launched an investigation to determine the extent of Wood's involvement, and Ernest Pitman committed suicide.

Asked by reporters to respond to the accusations, William Wood stated, "I cannot conceive what information could have been presented. . . . which in any way connected me with the so-called 'dynamite plot.'"

On May 19, 1913, Wood arrived at the Superior Courthouse in Boston to be tried for conspiracy to plant dynamite. At the trial's end he was acquitted.

As he exited the courthouse, Wood told reporters: "I am profoundly grateful for the verdict. . . . I had no reason at any time to assume that the verdict would be otherwise. I was not conscious of any guilt in connection with the alleged conspiracy because I was in no way implicated in it nor did I have any knowledge of it."

In 1914, AWC lost money for the first time, but the United States' entry into World War I in 1917 brought the company, and William Wood, lucrative government contracts to supply uniforms for the American military. American Woolen enjoyed enormous profits once more, but in contrast to the years before the 1912 strike, William Wood gave his workers frequent raises. In years to follow, Wood's workers were also given health insurance, maternity benefits, and sick leave. His company managers helped workers buy homes and arranged English languages classes for immigrants. Wood took the actions because he was determined to keep labor unions, such as the IWW, from organizing again in Lawrence.

William Wood made such significant changes in his company's policy toward its employees in the years after the great textile mill strike that he was no longer hated by his workers. But Wood's life did not have a happy ending. His empire began to fall apart in the 1920s, when shareholders of his company disagreed with many of his business decisions. He was forced to resign in 1924. On a vacation in Florida two years later, he asked his chauffeur to drive to an isolated area. He climbed out of the car, and after telling the driver to wait in the car, William Wood walked out of sight and shot himself.

Almost a century has passed since the Lawrence Strike of 1912 and many changes have taken place within the city's borders. The massive textile mills of the early twentieth century no longer operate in the expansive brick buildings that

The Merrimack River as it looked in 2005 when it overflowed its bank. Lawrence is in the background. *(Courtesy of the Associated Press)*

Immigrants' rights remain an issue in the United States. *(Courtesy of the Associated Press)*

remain along the banks of the Merrimack River. The men, women, and children who ran the dangerous textile machines and marched in the strike's picket lines, have long since passed away. Even the name of the strike has changed with the passage of time. Old timers called it The Lawrence Strike or simply The Strike; today, it's poetically remembered as the Bread and Roses Strike.

Yet, some things are the same in the city founded by Abbot Lawrence and the Essex Company. People from around the world still settle in Lawrence in the hope of pursuing the American Dream. Companies, today focusing on everything from technology to retail, use the old textile buildings as their bases of operation. And, although whistles and bells no longer signal the start of workdays for the big wool operations of men like William Wood, manufacturing still accounts for 35 percent of Lawrence's economy.

The Lawrence Strike of 1912 was an important milestone in the story of the American worker. Its successful conclusion demonstrated the importance of unions in a capitalist economy. It focused national attention on issues such as child labor, workplace safety, and the need for minimum-wage laws. Leaders in the United States government became more aware that laborers required laws to ensure they had food to eat and time to enjoy life—it could no longer be left up to the owners alone to make sure the workers earned enough to live a decent life. Workers, in other words, did deserve bread and roses.

Men and women like Ettor, Giovannitti, Flynn, Haywood, and William Wood gave the Lawrence Strike of 1912 its voice and its leadership. They provided strategies and carried out the negotiations in what became a national battleground between an American union and an American industry over the rights of American workers. But before the speeches and newspaper reports and photographs, before Congress turned a belated eye on labor issues, it was the hardworking immigrant laborers in Lawrence who risked their jobs, their homes, and their lives to strike for more pay and better work conditions.

"All the laws made for the betterment of workers' lives have their origin with the workers," noted journalist Mary Heaton Vorse. "Hours are shortened, wages go up, conditions are better—only if the workers protest."

From the beginning of the American Industrial Revolution, questions were asked about the relationship between business owners, business workers, and the United States government. Do workers have rights in the workplace? Do business owners have responsibilities to those they employ? Should the federal government play a role in regulating industry? The men who controlled the money that powered the early United States' industrial economy had insisted the answer to each question was no, and for years the majority of the public and the politicians had agreed with them. But during the Lawrence Strike of 1912, twenty-five thousand textile mill workers stood up and insisted that the country take another look at the issue. The result was a dramatic change in the American mind.

It was not the first time employees staged a strike against powerful employers. But this time, in the shadows of the mighty New England textile mills, an unexpected thing happened. The workers won.

2003 photo of Lawrence, Massachusetts *(Courtesy of the Associated Press)*

Bread and Roses

By James Oppenheim

As we come marching, marching, in the beauty of the day,
A million darkened kitchens, a thousand mill lofts gray,
Are touched with all the radiance that a sudden sun
discloses,
For the people hear us singing: "Bread and roses! Bread and
roses!

As we come marching, marching, we battle too for men,
For they are women's children, and we mother them again.
Our lives shall not be sweated from birth until life closes;
Hearts starve as well as bodies; give us bread, but give us
roses!

As we come marching, marching, unnumbered women dead
Go crying through our singing their ancient cry for bread.
Small art and love and beauty their drudging spirits knew.
Yes, it is bread we fight for—but we fight for roses, too.

As we come marching, marching, we bring the greater days.
The rising of the women means the rising of the race.
No more the drudge and idler—ten that toil where one
reposes,
But a share of life's glories: Bread and roses! Bread and roses!

This poem was published in American Magazine in December 1911. It became associated with the Lawrence Strike in 1916, when the poem was included in the pro-labor anthology, The Cry For Justice: An Anthology of the Literature of Social Protest, edited by Upton Sinclair, who connected the poem to struggle of the women in Lawrence. Though the Bread and Roses imagery has been become indelibly connected to the Lawrence Strike, some historians doubt that the strikers ever carried the signs that claimed they wanted "Bread and Roses, too." Regardless, the image has taken on its own significance, and adds a poetic and romantic aspect to the victory in Lawrence.

A textile worker steaming cloth *(Library of Congress)*

Timeline

1912

JANUARY **1** New Massachusetts labor law reduces workweek from fifty-six hours to fifty-four.

11 Polish workers walk off jobs; others join.

12 Strike officially declared; telegram sent to IWW's NY office.

13 Ettor gives first speech to strikers; strike committees form.

14 Mayor orders militia to report to state armory in Lawrence.

19 Mayor announces that no end is in sight for strike.

20 More militia arrive; estimated 20,000 on strike; police discover dynamite; Giovannitti and Flynn arrive.

21 Mill owners offer to meet with strikers based on individual mills; strike committee rejects.

24 Haywood arrives; strike committee meets with mill reps without owners.

26 Wood agrees to meet with Ettor.

27	Agents from AWC visit tenements announcing strike has ended; Ettor furious.
29	Mob attacks streetcars; LoPizzo is shot; Breen is arrested in dynamite plot.
30	Ramy dies from bayonet wound; Ettor and Giovannitti are arrested.
FEBRUARY 2	Strikers number between 23,000 and 25,000.
10	Flynn organizes 150 children and sends them to New York.
12	Strikers form first moving picket lines; approximately 3,000 begin returning to jobs.
17	One hundred and fifty children sent to New York and Barre, VT; Sweetzer warns IWW not to send kids without parents' consent.
22	Eleven children are prevented from going to Connecticut; Sullivan orders that no more children leave.
24	Forty children are stopped from departing for Philadelphia; riot leads to arrests of children and parents.
26	Haywood receives telegram to send strikers to Washington, D.C.
27	Arrested parents and children are reunited and charges dropped.

28 Mayor pleads with owners to concede to strikers.

MARCH 1 Strikers travel to Washington, D.C.; mill owners offer 5 percent raise.

2 Congressional hearings begin.

7 Congress vows further investigation into mills; forty-one children leave Lawrence for Philidelphia; owners negotiate with Committee of Ten.

9 Committee of Ten refuses Wood's proposed raises; fifteen children are sent to Manchester, NH.

12 Agreement is reached between Wood and Committee of Ten.

14 Strikers vote to accept terms and return to work.

24 Strike over in all mills; strike committee is voted out of existence.

27 Congress drops plans for further investigation.

30 Children return home.

APRIL Ettor and Giovannitti are indicted; Caruso is indicted for conspiring to kill LoPizzo; unknown man is accused of firing fatal bullet.

Sources

CHAPTER ONE: A City At War

p. 14, "If any of you women . . ." "Police Prevent Children's Exile," *The Lawrence Evening Tribune,* February 24, 1912.

p. 14, "I zend dem to mine friends!" Bruce Watson, *Bread and Roses* (New York: Viking, 2005), 168.

p. 14, "I want rights . . ." "Police and the Strikers Clash," *Lawrence Telegram,* February 24, 1912.

p. 15, "Police no good," Ibid.

p. 17, "Never before . . ." "United States May Intervene," *Boston Globe,* February 25, 1912.

CHAPTER TWO: Building an Industrial City

p. 26, "I came to America. . ." Watson, *Bread and Roses,* 7.

p. 27, "occupy so fully the lots . . ." *Report on the Strike of Textile Workers, 62nd Cong., 2d sess., 1912, H. Doc. 870, 146.*

p. 28, "fire risk . . ." Ibid., 151.

p. 31, "It makes one's blood boil . . ." "Operatives of All Races Making Common Cause," *The Leader,* January 21, 1912.

CHAPTER THREE: Building an Industrial Empire

p. 34, "When my father died . . ." Keene Sumner, "A Business Genius Who Has Done What Others Said Was Impossible," *American Magazine*, 1923, 203.

p. 34, "I asked questions of everybody . . ." Ibid.

p. 37, "Dad never was able . . ." Cornelius Wood, unpublished memoirs, (Lowell, MA: American Textile History Museum) Box 5, Folder 4, 155.

CHAPTER FOUR: Fighting for Bread and Roses

p. 43, "The grown-up workers . . ." Fred E. Beal, *Proletarian Journey* (New York: Da Capo Press, 1971), 37.

p. 43, "Short pay!" William Moran, *The Belles of New England* (New York: St. Martin's Press, 2002), 171.

p. 44, "Strike on in Lawrence . . ." "New Police Head for Lawrence," *Boston Globe*, February 20, 1912, 2.

p. 46, "The working class . . ." Watson, *Bread and Roses*, 55.

p. 46, "On this Friday morning . . ." Beal, *Proletarian Journey*, 38.

p. 47, "The threat of not being able . . ." Ibid., 39.

p. 47, "A tall Syrian worker . . ." Ibid., 40.

p. 48, "Better to starve fighting . . ." Philip S. Foner, *History of the Labor Movement in the United States*, (New York: International Publishers, Vol. IV, 1965), 316.

p. 49, "The manufacturers are the friends . . ." "A Statement by President Wood," *Lawrence Daily American*, January 12, 1912.

CHAPTER FIVE: The Imported Agitator

p. 54, "As long as the workers . . ." Watson, *Bread and*

Roses, 54.

p. 54, "ignorant and easily deceived . . ." "Mob Runs Riot in Mills at Lawrence," *Boston Globe*, January 13, 1912.

p. 55, "All that I ask . . ." "Strikers Firm and Mills May Close," *Boston Globe*, January 14, 1912.

p. 56, "Fifty cents buys ten loaves . . ." "Meeting Held in the City Hall This Afternoon," *Lawrence Telegram*, January 13, 1912.

p. 56, "Monday morning . . ." Watson, *Bread and Roses*, 66.

p. 58, "We desire peace . . ." "Militia Called at Lawrence," *Boston Globe*, January 15, 1912.

p. 60, "The pressure was so great . . ." Walter M. Pratt, "The Lawrence Revolution," *New England Magazine,* March 1912, 8.

p. 61, "You may turn your hose . . ." "The Strikers at Lawrence," *The Outlook*, February 10, 1912, 311.

p. 61, "Don't you think, Mr. Ettor . . ." "Strikers Driven Back by Troops but Close Mills, *Boston Globe*, January 16, 1912.

p. 62, "I am responsible . . ." Ibid.

p. 62-63, "I believe . . ." Ibid.

p. 63, "I shall stay here . . ." Ibid.

p. 63, "imported agitator," Watson, *Bread and Roses*, 67.

p. 63, "instigator of violence," Ibid.

p. 63, "They would jail me . . ." "Mass Meeting in the City Hall," *Lawrence Telegram*, January 16, 1912.

p. 63, "Things were so unusually quiet . . ." Pratt, "The Lawrence Revolution," 9-10.

CHAPTER SIX: A New Kind of Strike

p. 65, "Arise ye workers . . ." Watson, *Bread and Roses*, 78.

p. 67, "If any dynamite is found . . ." "No Dynamite in

Ettor's Suitcase," *The Lawrence Daily American*, January 22, 1912.

p. 68, "Our Employees..." "Statement of W.M. Wood Pres. Amer. Woolen Co.," *The Lawrence Daily American*, January 20, 1912.

p. 70, "To President William M. Wood . . ." "Strikers' Committee to the American Woolen Company," *The Lawrence Daily American*, January 22, 1912.

p. 70, "It was a new kind of strike . . ." Mary Heaton Vorse, *A Footnote to Folly: Reminiscences of Mary Heaton Vorse*, (New York: Farrar and Rhinehart, 1935), 5.

p. 71, "We [the militia] are going to look . . ." "The Massachusetts Labor Movement Collective Voices: The Textile Strike of 1912," (Boston, MA: Commonwealth Museum, 1998), 77.

p. 72, "We came to America . . ." "Strikers are Leaving City," *Lawrence Tribune*, February 5, 1912.

p. 72, "undesirable citizen," Watson, *Bread and Roses*, 94.

p. 73, "I hadn't realized . . ." Beal, *Proletarian Journey*, 47.

p. 75, "Mr. Wood told me . . ." "Pres. Wood and Directors Confer with Ettor," *The Lawrence Daily American*, January 27, 1912.

p. 75, "I was held up to the public . . ." Sumner, "A Business Genius Who Has Done What Others Said Was Impossible," *American Magazine*, 208.

p. 75, "If an overseer comes . . ." Watson, *Bread and Roses*, 103.

p. 76, "If they starve us . . ." "Shift in Plans of Workers' Chief," *Boston Globe*, sec. 2, January 28, 1912.

p. 76, "This town won't be very happy . . ." Watson,

Bread and Roses, 104.
p. 76, "Scab!" Ibid.

CHAPTER SEVEN: War Measures

p. 78, "before the fact of murder," "Ettor Not to Be
Released," *Boston Globe*, February 7, 1912.
p. 79, "are afraid to shoot . . ." "Will Shoot if Necessary,"
The Lawrence Daily American, January 30,
1912.
p. 81, "Why not have arrested . . ." "The Lawrence Strike:
A Poll of the Press," *The Outlook*, February 17, 1912,
357.
p. 82, "They say the strike is over . . ." "Haywood
Gives Out Statement," *The Lawrence Daily
American*, February 2, 1912.
p. 83, "Help Your Fellow Workers . . ." *Report of Strike
of Textile Workers in Lawrence, 1912*, 62nd
Cong., 2d sess., 1912, 496-497.
p. 84, "The strike is won if you . . ." Watson, *Bread
and Roses*, 130.
p. 85, "Why make me the figurehead . . ." Ibid., 139-140.
p. 87, "war measure," Ibid., 143.
p. 87, "Children of the Lawrence strikers . . ." Ibid.

CHAPTER EIGHT: National Scandal

p. 88-89, "We, the undersigned . . ." "Identification Card,"
Lawrence Telegram, February 24, 1912.
p. 90, "When Elizabeth Gurley Flynn spoke . . ."
Watson, *Bread and Roses*, 155.
p. 90, "good old Massachusetts . . ." Margaret Sanger,
"The Fighting Women of Lawrence," *The Public
Papers of Margaret Sanger: Web Edition*, http://
wilde.acs.its.nyu.edu/sanger/documents/

show.php?sangerDoc=304679.xml (accessed November, 15 2006).

p. 90, "Sure, good old Massachusetts!" Ibid.

p. 92, "Who are we?" "150 Waifs Find Homes Here," *New York Times*, February 11, 1912.

p. 92-93, "Almost all snatched at their food . . ." Margaret Sanger, *An Autobiography*, (New York: W.W. Norton and Company, 1938), 82.

p. 93, "I could scarcely believe . . ." Watson, *Bread and Roses*, 145-146.

p. 93, "Did you see a woman . . . a policeman" "Defense Scores," *Boston Globe*, February 21, 1912.

p. 94, "Their garments were simply worn . . ." Sanger, *An Autobiography*, 81.

p. 95, "Usually a night-stick . . ." Elizabeth Gurley Flynn, *I Speak My Own Piece: The Autobiography of the Rebel Girl*, (New York: Masses and Mainstream, 1955), 126.

p. 95, "There will be no more . . ." "Children to be Kept at Home," *The Lawrence Evening Tribune*, February 22, 1912.

p. 95, "I will not hesitate . . ." Ibid.

p. 97, "I saw the soldiers . . ." "Congressmen Hear Strikers' Children," *New York Times*, March 5, 1912.

p. 97, "to the world that we are able . . ." Watson, *Bread and Roses*, 170.

p. 99, "The Lawrence authorities . . ." Ibid., 175.

p. 99, "All this occurred . . ." Ibid.

p. 99, "lost their heads" Ibid., 175-76.

CHAPTER NINE: Congressional Hearing

p. 100, "have starved the workers . . ." "Strikers

Proclaim," *Lawrence Evening Tribune,*
February 27, 1912

p. 101, "many conflicts between capital and labor . . ."
Watson, *Bread and Roses*, 185.

p. 103, "would not yield pennies . . ." Ibid., 182-183.

p. 104, "I have here from Lawrence . . ." *Hearings Before
the Committee on Rules of the House of
Representatives*, House Resolutions 409
and 433, (Washington, D.C., March 2-7, 1912).

p. 104-106, "Why did you go . . . certainly" Ibid., 32-51.

p. 107, "It happened . . . seven years old" Ibid.

p. 111-113, "Camella, how old . . . enough to eat at home"
Ibid., 169-172.

p. 114-115, "You stated this morning . . . their best ribbons"
Ibid., 232-233.

p. 115, "I have seen worse clad people . . ." "Haywood to
Take Stand in Washington," *The Lawrence
Daily American*, March 7, 1912.

p. 115, "Yes, but you never saw . . ." Ibid.

p. 116, "Those that are idle . . ." Watson, *Bread and
Roses*, 196.

CHAPTER TEN: The End of the Strike

p. 121, "You, the strikers of Lawrence . . ." "Strike
Committee Approves of the Advance in Wages
Offered by American Woolen Company,"
Lawrence Evening Tribune, March 13, 1912.

p. 126, "guilty of nothing except . . ." William Haywood,
*Bill Haywood's Book: The Autobiography of William
D. Haywood*, (New York: International
Publishers, 1929), 256.

p. 128, "The Second Battle of Lawrence." Foner, *History
of the Labor Movement*, 344-345.

p. 130, "I have not been tried . . ." Watson, *Bread and Roses*, 236-237.

p. 131, "What about the better . . ." Ibid., 237.

p. 131, "working class," "Acquitted, They Kissed," *New York Times*, November 27, 1912.

p. 131, "in the name of justice . . ." Ibid.

p. 131, "he didn't do it" "Not Guilty, For All," *Boston Globe*, November 27, 1912.

CHAPTER ELEVEN: Immigrant City

p. 135, "approved . . ." "Strike Expense Account Figures," *Lawrence Telegram*, May 23, 1913.

p. 136, "I cannot conceive . . ." Watson, *Bread and Roses*, 222.

p. 136, "I am profoundly grateful . . ." Edward G. Roddy, *Mills, Mansions, and Mergers: The Life of William M. Wood*, (North Andover, MA: Merrimack Valley Textile Museum, 1921), 73-74.

p. 139, "All the laws made . . ." Mary Heaton Vorse, *A Footnote to Folly*, 11.

Bibliography

Beal, Fred E. *Proletarian Journey.* New York: Da Capo
Press, 1971.

Flynn, Elizabeth Gurley. "Memories of the Industrial
Workers
of the World (IWW)." Address to Students and
Faculty Members of Northern Illinois University,
DeKalb, November 8, 1962.

———. *I Speak My Own Piece: The Autobiography of the
Rebel Girl.* New York: Masses and Mainstream, 1955.

Foner, Philip S. *History of the Labor Movement in the
United States.* New York: International Publishers,
Vol. IV, 1965.

Haywood, William D. *Bill Haywood's Book:
The Autobiography of William D. Haywood.* New York:
International Publishers, 1929.

U.S. Congress. House. *Hearings Before the Committee on Rules of the House of Representatives on House Resolutions 409 and 433.* 62nd Congress, 2nd sess., H. Doc. 671.

Moran, William. *The Belles of New England.* New York: St. Martin's Press, 2002.

Pratt, Walter M. "The Lawrence Revolution." *New England Magazine,* March 1912.

U.S. Congress. House. *Report on the Strike of Textile Workers,* 62nd Congress, 2nd sess., H Doc. 870.

Roddy, Edward. *Mills, Mansions, and Mergers: The Life of William M. Wood.* North Andover, MA: Merrimack Valley Textile Museum, 1921.

Sanger, Margaret. *An Autobiography.* New York: W.W. Norton and Company, 1938.

———. "The Fighting Women of Lawrence." *The Public Papers of Margaret Sanger: Web Edition.* http://wilde. acs. its.nyu.edu/sanger/documents/ show.php?sangerDoc=3 04679.xml (accessed November 15, 2006).

Sumner, Keene. "A Business Genius Who Has Done What Others Said Was Impossible." *American Magazine,* June 1923, 203.

"The Lawrence Strike: A Poll of the Press," *The Outlook,* February 17, 1912, 357.

"The Massachusetts Labor Movement Collective Voices: The Textile Strike of 1912," (Boston, MA: Commonwealth Museum, 1998), 77.

Weyl, Walker E. "The Strikers at Lawrence," *The Outlook,* February 10, 1912, 309-12.

Vorse, Mary Heaton. "Lawrence Strike." *A Footnote to*

Folly: Reminiscences of Mary Heaton Vorse. New York: Farrar and Rhinehart, 1935. Also available online at http://www.marxists.org/subject/women/authors/vorse/index.html.

Watson, Bruce. *Bread and Roses.* New York: Viking, 2005

Wood, Cornelius. "Unpublished Memoirs." Lowell, MA: American Textile History Museum, Box 5, Folder 4, 155.

Web sites

http://www.iww.org/en/culture
Official Web site of the IWW, focusing on the history of the organization, its impact, and its current activities.

http://www.cityoflawrence.com/Pages/index
Official Web site of the city of Lawrence, Massachusetts. In addition to a page on the city's history, the site features information and photos about the "Immigrant City" today.

http://digital.library.arizona.edu/bisbee/docs/131.php
The full text of an essay by Joseph Ettor entitled "Industrial Unionism: The Road to Freedom."

Index